Worry Free RETIREMENT

DO WHAT YOU WANT
WHEN YOU WANT
WHERE YOU WANT

Brian Fricke, CFP

Advantage®

Published by Advantage, Charleston, South Carolina.
Member of Advantage Media Group.

ADVANTAGE is a registered trademark and the Advantage colophon is a trademark of Advantage Media Group, Inc.

Printed in the United States of America.

ISBN: 978-1-59932-085-4
LCCN: 2008936316

Most Advantage Media Group titles are available at special quantity discounts for bulk purchases for sales promotions, premiums, fundraising, and educational use. Special versions or book excerpts can also be created to fit specific needs.

For more information, please write: Special Markets, Advantage Media Group, P.O. Box 272, Charleston, SC 29402 or call 1.866.775.1696.

Cover illustration by Chris Scott [cscott@hardwaystudios.com].

TABLE OF CONTENTS

ACKNOWLEDGEMENTS

My wife is always teasing me that I live a charmed life. And you know what? She's right!

I owe it all to God, my family, and everyone who has in some way come into my life. Words can never tell you how deeply thankful I am.

To my wife, Annette, for always trusting and believing in me. Sometimes grabbing me by the ankles and bringing me back down to earth.

To everyone affiliated with our financial planning firm, Financial Management Concepts. Clients, staff and strategic partners—because of our relationship I am able to live my life today, "Doing what I want, when I want, where I want!"

And, especially for the good fortune of being an American and living in the United States of America, I know of no other place in the world that allows a person to pursue their dreams and create a life for themselves and their family of their own choosing.

WHY YOU SHOULD LISTEN TO ME

You've opened this book because you have some questions about your finances. But, why listen to me? There are thousands of investing and personal finance books by journalists, advisors and other "experts."

I want you to feel both comfortable and confident that I have the knowledge and experience that will help you. I've seen the devastating consequences when clients are financially ruined by a health emergency, a failing business or other crises. Proper planning in advance will enable you to avoid such disasters.

I have been a Certified Financial Planner (CFP) for nearly twenty years. I've owned my own independent financial planning firm specializing in retirees and retirement related issues for the last eighteen years. *Wealth Manager Magazine* has recognized my company, Financial Management Concepts, as one of America's top wealth managers the last five years in a row, 2004 through 2008. Over the years, we have worked with more than 756 families. We've assisted our clients through virtually every type of financial planning event imaginable.

MY BACKGROUND

When my friends in high school asked about my plans for the future, I said I would be "rich." I wasn't being arrogant but I simply knew that I could become a millionaire. It didn't bother me in the least that I had absolutely no idea how I would accomplish my dream. I was certain that, at least for me, college was not the answer.

I guess deep down inside I always knew I would own a business. To this day, I remember my father always telling me, "Be the best at whatever you do. If you do that you'll always be well paid." I could hardly wait until the day when I could join my father in the family business.

Then the unthinkable happened—my father died. I was sixteen, he was forty-two. One week later, my mother went from being a "full-time mom" and part-time bookkeeper to a full-time business owner, with all the accompanying responsibility. Mom had no choice. She had to keep the company going to take care of her two boys.

In hindsight, I realize that this is one of the key reasons I do what I do. My mother should have had choices. She should have been able to decide what she wanted to do with her life, without money influencing her decision.

At age eighteen, I got my real estate license and started my career in residential real estate sales. I quickly learned that this field was not for me. I remember working with an investor who bought and sold rental homes and noticed his profits far exceeded my commissions, while I did the majority of the work. Soon after, I found myself buying and selling rental properties.

Then a funny thing started to happen. People began asking me how they could become financially successful. My future as a financial planner began.

I interviewed with every financial planning firm in town. These companies fell into two groups. One group was composed of insurance agents who were interested only in selling life insurance and the occasional disability policy. The other group of planners only wanted to sell investments. I just knew there had to be something better. I wanted to work with people and help them use the strategies that would give them choices. I wanted my clients to achieve their goals—such as raising a family, pursuing interests outside of their jobs and fulfilling other ambitions.

I remember coming home one evening and announcing with great enthusiasm to my wife that I would open my own financial planning company the following week. We had $20,000 in the bank, with an understanding that when that money was spent, I'd go back and get a "real job." We also had a three-month-old infant and my wife had recently quit her well paying job to be a full-time mom. This was a choice that we both felt (and still do) was very important to us.

I was on top of the world. I owned my own company! It didn't matter that I had no clients or income. My wife had absolute trust and confidence in me. With her support, I earned a Certified Financial Planner (CFP) designation. I didn't care about getting this accreditation but my wife pushed me to earn it.

I recall the afternoon we sat down together on our living room sofa to review our finances. There wasn't much to say—we had no savings, $30,000 of credit card debt, two cars and a house. It's also the day she announced we would be having our second child. It was apparently time for me to get "a real job."

But somehow, we stuck with my fledgling planning practice and hoped that our circumstances would change for the better. They did. My family and my company are totally debt free. We have raised two sons, both now well on their way to becoming outstanding young men.

In the fledgling days of my business, I took on everyone who approached me as a client. I worked very long hours and was hardly home. Eventually, as the company grew, I realized that I needed to restructure the business. Today, we handle a maximum of ninety-five clients, but we manage all of their financial decisions. This enables us to operate our business effectively—and it lets our clients spend their days doing what's important to them.

Along the way, I have found that my definition of being "rich" has changed. It's not about how much money I have accumulated but more about having the freedom and security to do what I want, when I want, and with whom I want. This, I truly believe, is what our company is all about.

We have clients who can walk away from millions of dollars in stock options, knowing they already "have enough." They're sacrificing what would be enticing to someone else by choosing to spend their time doing what matters to them. Another client has taken early retirement so he can pursue interesting opportunities like working with his church and organizing missions around the world.

None of our clients will show up on a list of the "Wealthiest Americans." However, I am certain that they are truly "richer" than many of the people on these lists.

You can find out more about me and my company at www.BrianFricke.com.

KNOW YOUR VALUES

Before you go to the grocery store, you make a list of what you need to buy. Once you're in the store, you might add some other items to your shopping cart but you definitely want to get certain items. When you're planning a vacation, you do legwork ahead of time. You buy a travel guide or look online for details about your destination, you comparison shop airfares and hotels, etc.

Planning ahead is simply a sensible strategy that helps you avoid stress. But somehow, when it comes to retirement planning, people often overlook this type of preparation. Perhaps, it is just too intimidating to plan for something that is so uncertain. Even discussing retirement can be confusing because your definition of the ideal retirement is unlikely to be the same as mine. Your notion of a "worry-free retirement" may not even be the same as your spouse's!

First, you need to define what retirement means—for you, not someone else. Retirement today is not the same as it was for your parents or grandparents when most people worked for the same company for twenty or thirty years and then stop working altogether. Many people now plan on working either part-time or in a new field after they have formally retired.

Defining retirement is closely related to another important consideration—knowing your values. Values are not the same as your

13

goals. Every time I meet with someone who is unhappy and dissatisfied with his or her financial situation, I can usually trace the issues back to decisions the individual made that were not aligned with his or her core values.

What do I mean by values? You need to identify and understand your core values. One of the first conversations we have with new clients is discussing what's important about money to them. The answers I get most often are related to safety, security and freedom. When we ask clients to explain these words, they generally respond that they don't want to worry and they want peace of mind. With peace of mind comes less stress. This in turn enables people to have a better outlook on life and overall, a healthier mental attitude. Furthermore, if you're feeling good about your own financial situation, you are then in a position to help other people (friends, family) financially and emotionally. For many people, this ability to help others is their reason for 'being.' Sometimes it means knowing they're living their life according to God's plan.

That's the heart of knowing your values. Everyone wants to know that their life has meaning, purpose, and passion. But you have to accept that you're not the same as the person who lives next door or works in the cubicle alongside you. Your first step is to think about your values and what's important to you. Once you fully appreciate your values, you can then begin to define your goals for the future.

WHY MOST PEOPLE FAIL AT SETTING GOALS

The single biggest mistake people make when they set goals is that their goals are too vague. Almost everyone says they want to have a million dollars. Why? "Well, if I had a million dollars and I earned 10%, I'd have $100,000 that I could spend and that would make for a pretty comfortable life." And why is that? "Well, I don't know," is the standard response.

The million dollar answer sounds appealing but if you can't even explain why you need that much money, then it will be difficult for you to have a worry-free retirement because you can't specify what you want to do or when you want to do it or where you want to do it. You need to be able to describe your ideal retirement image if you're going to get there!

Wouldn't it be a shame if—in order to live life on your terms doing what you want whenever you want wherever you want—you only needed $800,000 but you denied yourself that opportunity because you were waiting to grow your nest egg to $1 million. On the other hand, wouldn't it be a shame if you really needed $1.3 million and you started spending your nest egg when you hit $1 million only to find out later in life that you've run out of money but it's too late to return to work.

Before you can tackle the necessary decisions related to retirement including investments, taxes, insurance, etc, you must identify your values and then determine your goals and what you want to accomplish over your lifetime. The fun comes when you accomplish your goals and you have tangible evidence that you are living life according to *your* true values.

Here's what I mean by setting specific goals. "I want to retire when I'm fifty-five," is too vague. A specific goal would be "I want to retire when I'm fifty-five and for me that means January 1, 2017, with a monthly income of $5,000 after taxes or a yearly income of $60,000 net after taxes." That's a specific goal.

Another example of a concrete goal is not saying, "I want to travel." Instead, you might say, "I want to have $10,000 to $15,000 for travel per year. I want that money available and I want to start spending that money next year." You would write your goals and specify the year or the month, if possible, in which you want to start traveling and the year in which you will need to have the travel fund available

In order for you to have a valid goal, you must have something in writing. A goal is not simply something that you discuss with friends. It is an important objective and having it in writing also reminds you to handle the necessary financial, legal and tax issues that go along with your goal. Having written goals that you review periodically reminds you why you're doing certain things and helps you focus on what really matters.

Another benefit to writing your goals is that putting them on paper helps imprint them on your subconscious. Here's an example from my life:

My wife and I got married in 1986. At that time, we sat down and wrote down goals that we wanted to achieve. We wanted to have a nice home for when we started a family. We eventually wanted to have a condo at the beach, a cabin in the mountains, and an airplane. I dreamed of being able to fly my family back and forth from the beach to the mountains.

Fortunately, my wife and I are now in a position where we have achieved our goals: We have two kids; we have a nice home and we have the condo at the beach. The cabin in the mountains has turned into a town home. Along the way, we found out we don't like the maintenance and upkeep that a house requires, especially as we get closer to being empty nesters ourselves. The airplane has turned into a boat because it turns out our whole family likes being in and around water.

Both of our boys are avid surfers and yes, I surf too. My oldest son and I have a hobby of offshore fishing and we've even won a fishing tournament. So, we modified the airplane goal and turned it into a boat.

It's worth mentioning that your goals aren't static—I didn't expect to learn to love boating. Some of your goals may stay the same but others will vary as circumstances in your life change. While you may modify your goals, your core values don't disappear. Freedom, security, peace of mind, less stress, less worry, being able to help others whether it's your family or your spouse, giving back to the community, living life the way God intended you to live. Those are all examples of core values that rarely vary.

That's why you need to understand your core values before you set goals. With a clear vision of your values, you will be able to match your goals with your values. For example, my wife and I don't always agree. For example, she's not fond of offshore fishing. When we put a goal on our goal sheet or "financial roadmap," we both have to agree on the goal. She may not use or enjoy the same things as me but we have to agree on something that goes on our financial roadmap. Focusing on your core values always helps you gain clarity about your goals.

In fact, Roy Disney, Walt's brother, said, "When values are clear, decisions are easy." Most financial advisors would drool at the opportunity to have a multi-million dollar Lotto winner as a client. Not me. I have turned down not one but three different multi-million dollar Lotto winners. Why would I turn down these clients? The answer is really quite simple. None of these people had a clear vision of what was important to them. Their overriding concern at the time was hiring a planning firm that would get them the best rate of return for their money. But they hadn't given any thought to their core values. By the way, two years later, these Lotto winners had spent most of their newfound money and hadn't changed their way of life.

Who cares what rate of return you're getting if you're not living a life with purpose, meaning and passion? If you don't understand what a value-driven life is, you're never going to be happy, with or without the help of a financial advisor.

For more assistance defining and establishing your core values, I highly recommend the book, Values-Based Financial Planning: The Art of Creating an Inspiring Financial Strategy *by Bill Bachrach.*

THE NEW DEFINITION
OF RETIREMENT

Not too many years ago, the word "retirement" was associated with people spending hours on the golf course or traveling leisurely around the world. Today, the images of retirement aren't so promising. Increasing healthcare costs, recent declines in the stock market and the sub-prime mortgage crisis have all added to the concerns people have about their retirement, especially from a financial view. Fortunately, though, there are some reasons to be optimistic. People are living longer and in many cases, are healthier, thanks to lifestyle changes and advances in medical care. Also, the notion at age sixty-five, you must stop working and move to a retirement community is out-of-date. There is no universal definition of "retirement" that meets everyone's needs.

What's important is that you take charge of planning for your retirement so that you can enjoy it to the fullest. Some things like an unexpected health crisis are not in your control but planning for travel, a new career, volunteer work, etc. are all within your power! I tell my clients to strive for a worry-free retirement. This means that you will be able to "Do what you want, when you want and where you want." An increasing number of people are choosing to continue working beyond 'normal retirement age'. Not because they *have to*, but because they *want to*. Some will even trade in one career for new employment opportunities.

I consider myself retired because I'm in the position of being able to do what I want, when I want and where I want. I'm still working because my business brings me purpose and passion. If you're fortunate enough to have a position that also brings you great satisfaction, consider yourself lucky and don't think about giving it up. If you're living and leading a balanced life, keep doing so.

Here are some examples of how our clients handled their retirement plans:

Several years ago, John accepted an early retirement package. About six months into retirement, he called me in a panic. His former employer had contacted him to see if he would be willing to work on a project as an independent contractor. John thought it would take three to four months to complete. His primary concern was how this extra income, if he accepted the project, would affect his Social Security benefits.

Before answering his question, I asked him if doing this work would bring joy and satisfaction in to his life. John told me that he had finished all his "retirement" projects and was starting to get a little bored. While the opportunity seemed interesting, he was concerned for his wife, Wanda, as it would require him living overseas for three or four months. I asked John whether his wife might want to visit and spend time with him overseas. He was sure that she would like this opportunity but he wasn't convinced that the company would pay the additional expense.

I recommended that he let his former employer know that he would be willing to accept the assignment if the company was willing to accept his terms. I told John to be ready for either an initial turn down or possibly a delayed response. John asked the company to fly him and his wife first class and provide them with a Marriott-type quality level hotel suite. I also advised him to ask for a daily fee that was 30% higher than his previous salary, if calculated on a daily basis. My reasoning was that the firm was still saving money because John was no longer an employee and the company was saving this 30% because the company wouldn't be paying Social Security and Medicare taxes as well as other employee benefits.

Sure enough, John's initial request was turned down. However, a week later his contact called back to see if he was still interested at his original terms. As it turned out his immediate supervisor only had financial authority up to a certain level. So he had to get permission "from above," which he had hoped to avoid.

That was nearly ten years ago and John is still doing project work for his former employer and has no plans to quit. He occasionally turns down projects that conflict with his personal travel plans or if he doesn't like the project. The last time we spoke John commented that he's having more fun now than ever. I'm not surprised. People are generally happier when they feel that they're in control of their time.

When the company Kathy worked for went public, the stock shot up like a rocket. Her stock options and retirement plan were now worth several million dollars. This was more than enough money for her and her husband to enjoy life like they had always envisioned. Although the couple were relatively young, not quite age 50, they didn't want to work at all. Instead, they a bought a brand new 48-foot sport fishing boat. David even got his captain's license. They've cruised all over the Bahamas, the Caribbean and Florida Keys, sometimes by themselves and other times with friends and family. That was nearly a decade ago and recently, they've put the boat up for sale. They are looking forward to the next chapter in their lives, though they're not certain what it will be. Fortunately, they've made smart investment decisions and will never have to return to work for financial reasons.

Nine years ago Danny accepted an early retirement offer and since then he's been spending most of his time in a national leadership role with his church. When he's not involved with his voluntary unpaid "church business," Danny and his wife Carolyn spend time traveling or visiting their children and grandchildren. More importantly, they are living their lives with a sense of purpose and passion.

Over the years, I've observed that my retired clients who stay active and involved, whether it's working part-time, volunteering for their church or another charity they care about, traveling and pursuing hobbies, all end up having a happier and more fulfilling life. Also, their lives are a lot less stressful than when they worked full-time. As a group, their health is significantly better compared to other people who have retired but don't do much other than sit on the couch.

No matter how you choose to define your "worry free retirement," make sure you stay active and involved. By doing so, you are guaranteed to lead a life filled with purpose and passion!

Note: For more stories about people enjoying their own version of a "worry free retirement" go to www.BrianFricke.com.

THE FINANCIAL MEDIA IS NOT YOUR FRIEND

When I look at the offerings of the financial media today—radio, TV, print or online—I always feel as if I'm somehow inferior because I'm not on top of the latest news about investing. I can only imagine how guilty people who aren't financial professionals feel—all because of the business press!

Financial journalists advocate becoming an "expert" on all subjects. If you're taking out a mortgage, then you need to know not just everything about mortgages, but also everything about homes and house repair. And, if you're taking out a car loan, then you need to know everything about car repairs and in fact, how cars are assembled. I don't know about you, but I've intentionally chosen not to spend my time learning all this drivel. Some of you may find doing all this research enjoyable and rewarding, but I'm definitely not in that camp. I simply don't listen to radio or TV programs on car repair and I don't read any magazines about cars.

Since I've decided that I don't want to know how a car is built, I have also chosen not to do any of my own repairs, including changing the oil. Instead, I have found a mechanic who I trust. I believe that he is an expert at his work and, furthermore, he's not going to cheat me.

That's why I find it incredible that so many people treat the financial media as if they're trusted advisors. The reality is that the primary goal of the financial media is not to educate you. The publications or programs have to make a profit. They have to sell advertising, which is accomplished by delivering more viewers/readers for their advertisers.

I derive no satisfaction in fixing my car. All I want to do is turn the key and have it get me from point A to point B. You need to be brutally honest with yourself when it comes to money and finance. If you love calculations, following the stock listings, comparison shopping on insurance policies, monitoring the latest tax regulations, that's terrific. In fact, with the Internet, it's easier than ever for you to keep up with all these financial details. But, most of you should let a trusted advisor do the legwork and research for you...

THE MAGAZINE COVER INDICATOR

My colleagues and I have been monitoring a trend we call "The Magazine Cover Indicator." Simply put, we have observed that whenever something finally makes it to the cover of a magazine, the move has typically run its course and the stock or sector is ready to head in the other direction. For example, if a magazine headline is touting a particular company, the stock of that company has already rallied and is overpriced. Conversely, if the headline is negative about a certain sector or company, nearly everyone who wanted to sell has already sold.

While I can't statistically prove that the magazines are always wrong or late with their predictions, we have looked at a number of magazines. When we look back at the covers, we've found that you would have had higher returns if you did the exact opposite of the magazine's advice. Look at this sampling below from several magazines:

Two recent covers featuring the international markets caught our eye. First, *Business Week* came out with a cover story, "The Trouble with India" and *The Economist's* cover story was labeled, "Europe's mid-life crisis." Both of these covers have negative implications for these countries. This was interesting since the US markets continue to have weak demand (meaning relative strength) compared to the international markets. In fact, as of December 2007, all our international holdings have outperformed the US holdings, on a year to date basis. In case you're wondering, our US holdings are still outperforming the Dow and the S&P 500. But you should understand why we have been favoring international stocks in our portfolios.

If you're one of my clients, you know that I hate when you bring me in clippings from newspapers or magazines. You're excited by the prospect of high returns because of what you've read. Unfortunately, by the time you're reading about some "hot new stock or development" whoever wanted "in," is already in. This means demand has probably started to weaken. If there isn't going to be increasing demand (which indicates relative strength) then odds are the prices and values aren't going to go up much either!

Remember, don't trust a magazine cover! If you enjoy learning about investments and the world economy, there are many media outlets that you can choose from. Just don't assume that you're always getting reliable information.

1 Year Later Look at Some Magazine Covers

February 20, 2006
1 Year Later: GM +64%

October 2, 2004
1 Year Later: EFA +22%

September 14, 1998
1 Year Later: SPX +30%

February 12, 2001
1 Year Later: Not Trading

October 25, 2003
1 Year Later: Crude +80%

December 27, 1999
1 Year Later: AMZN -79%

THE SINGLE BIGGEST
MONEY MISTAKE

Recently, I met with Joe who was thinking about hiring us. Joe had decided that he wanted to handle everything himself. Quite frankly, he had done a really good job on his own. I told him that. I could understand why he was having trouble justifying hiring us. Joe was pretty sure he could do it all himself. "That's great, Joe. What about Helen?" I asked. My point was that if something happened to Joe, his wife and children needed to be in a position to deal with the estate. Wouldn't it make more sense for Joe to work with us to make decisions now so that his wife and children wouldn't have to be making them later on during a stressful time?

In fact, this situation is quite common. Many spouses assume certain roles so that one person tends to make more of the financial decisions themselves, excluding their spouses from the process and unfortunately, sometimes keeping important information from their family.

Here's another example: Mary, a very wise and knowledgeable investor, would come and visit with me about every year or so but would never hire us. She was managing her money pretty well and I suspect she just wasn't comfortable with paying me or anyone else for that matter, for financial advice. Her husband Mark had absolutely no interest in money or finances. He was a retired military man and was happy knowing that he always had his monthly "allowance" in his pocket and that all their bills were always paid. The couple owed no one. They didn't have a mortgage. Mark was very proud of Mary and the excellent job she had done, not only raising their children, managing the household, but also in taking responsibility for all their financial affairs.

Then one day, Mark called me and I immediately knew something wasn't right. Since Mark would always delegate any financial/money issues to Mary, he would never call a financial advisor. Mark was very distressed and told me that Mary had passed away two weeks earlier. On her deathbed, Mary had told Mark not to worry about anything and to call me. She had said that, "I would take care of him." Well... the couple had two grown children—a daughter who had been estranged from the family for many years, and a son with bipolar disorder which is managed with medication but who will always require a certain level of supervision

When Mark came in to meet with me for the first time, he brought in a stack of thirty-seven envelopes, one on top of the other. This stack—exactly 5¾" high—consisted of empty envelopes from thirty-seven different mutual fund and investment companies. Mark was pretty sure they had money invested with all of these companies, but he had no idea where the monthly statements were or how much was in any of the accounts. Needless to say, he had no idea what the statements looked like let alone how to even read one.

This is where we started. One of my colleagues spent two and a half days at Mark's home, going through all his legal and financial papers. Fortunately, the couple did have a little over $1 million, in addition to their home. Along with Mark's military pension and Social Security, there will be more than enough money to take care of Mark and his special needs son.

Don't think this is an isolated situation. Just recently, my wife ran into a family friend at the grocery store. The two women caught each other up on the latest family news. Diana was telling my wife about a medical scare with her husband Rob. As he was being prepared for serious back surgery, he told Diana that she should call me if he didn't make it through the operation! In fact, while I had met the couple six or seven years before, I was not familiar with their finances. Like other couples, Diana let Rob handle all the financial matters for the family.

What do Mary and Rob have in common? They each have spouses who have little or no knowledge or the desire to learn about their financial matters. As a result, Mary and Rob made the financial decisions without consulting their spouses. The real problem comes when the uninterested spouse—as with Mark—suddenly has to take charge of the family finances when the other person gets ill or dies. The absolute worst type of client a financial advisor could ever have is a newly widowed spouse who has never taken any interest in the household investments and is now left alone to make investing decisions. It's good that they're seeking the advice of a financial advisor, but even finding the right advisor can be a scary decision. They're just not comfortable handling any type of financial decision, especially if they have just lost their trusted spouse.

If you love your spouse, do him or her a favor—start working with a financial advisor now! You should find an advisor whom you both like and trust. That way, when your spouse is left alone, he or she will already have a trusted financial advisor in place. This will reduce the stress the surviving spouse feels. This is one of the best legacies you can ever give your spouse and one he or she will always be grateful for.

THE SECRET TO A SUCCESSFUL INVESTMENT STRATEGY

Without fail, the single biggest financial mistake you can make is not having a written investment strategy. This game plan reflects your principles, values and philosophies about your finances. You, or your advisor, need to have this strategy in a written form.

You'll rarely refer to this document during a bull market when your investments are increasing in value. On the other hand, when the market is going down and the value of your portfolio is less than you anticipated, the document will become invaluable.

During uncertain times, otherwise very rational people tend to make very irrational decisions because their emotions overwhelm their reasoning. That's why—whether you're managing your money on your own or you use an advisor—you need to have a written investment strategy in place. You can write your own but most people will work closely with their financial advisor to craft their statement. Don't be bullied into including any approach that doesn't match your values or beliefs. This is *your* investment philosophy, not someone else's.

By my estimates, more than 95% of individual investors don't have a written investment strategy and even some 85% of financial advisors don't use them. However, I believe they are invaluable and if your advisor doesn't work with you to create one, then it may be time to find an advisor who will.

ARE YOU WILLING TO LOOK STUPID?

No one wants to look stupid doing anything, especially choosing investments. You always want to make the right move at the right time. I'm going to let you in on a secret. Sooner or later, we all end up looking stupid. Even the most successful investors, end up looking stupid, at least some of the time. There's just no way around it! But you can minimize the chances of making foolish decisions by having an investment system. I've seen this with nearly every client over the past two decades. The key to succcessful investing is having a system.

Warren Buffett. You know the name. He's considered one of the most successful investors around. He's also one of the richest men in America, at least until recently, when he gave most of his fortune to charity, the Bill and Melinda Gates Foundation.

What's the secret to Buffett's success? Buffett is known as a "value" investor, from the style first discussed by Benjamin Graham. Buffett doesn't focus on the movement of the stock market at a particular point in time but instead, he looks at individual stocks and how well these companies are performing. Remember, back in the late 90s, when all the "smart money" was going into tech stocks, before the tech bubble burst? Tech stocks were never part of Buffett's portfolio despite criticism from so-called experts who said he was missing an enormous opportunity. What happened? Many investors lost millions because they bet on tech stocks but Buffett remains on top and his portfolio continues to grow and outperform the stock market.

Buffett was confident that his system was the right one and he stuck with it even when it appeared he was looking stupid. This is an important lesson. All successful investors have a system they believe in and they follow it over the long haul. There are times when they look stupid but that doesn't bother them!

You need to ask yourself whether you're following an investment system that you're confident in, even when it makes you look foolish. Trust me, if you haven't looked stupid yet, the time will come. And that's the time when you'll be most inclined to question your system. But you shouldn't. You need to have enough confidence in your system to stick to it even if everyone around you seems to have a different approach.

If you're already one of our members, you already have a system in place. You're using ours! If you're wondering, our system does make us look stupid on occasion. 2006 is a good example of one such time.

Our members' returns in January 2006 were eye-popping (2005 wasn't too bad either). But from February through August 2006, our system was making us look stupid. But since we believe in our system, we knew this period would be temporary. By the end of 2006, our system had recovered and our members ended up with respectable, albeit not eye-popping returns.

Whether you use our system, your own or someone else's, make sure you have a system and put in writing! Review your system to ensure that it's the right one for your financial situation. Stick with it, even when it makes you look stupid.

There's no doubt that you can make a great deal of money if you hold stock in a company that performs well over many years but having all your holdings in one company can also be a recipe for financial disaster if anything happens to that company's

WARNING

Going Overboard on Company Stock

If you've worked for one company for a long period of time, you probably feel pretty good about your employer. Furthermore, because of your longevity, you may hold a large portion of your investment portfolio in the company stock. While this may seem to be a sound investment strategy, it can be far less secure than you think. Over the past decade, many large companies have gone bankrupt, leaving many people without jobs but even more damaging, costing others the savings they worked so hard to accumulate over many years.

No doubt, you've heard of Enron, the Fortune 500 company now defunct. I'll never forget when friends came to see me. Jim, in his early forties, had worked for the company for his entire career. Virtually 99% of all his family's savings and investments were in Enron stock or stock options. At the time, this amounted to well over $2 million. Based on Jim's and, his wife, Melissa's goals, I said that they had already accumulated enough to accomplish their goals. Their primary risk was having all their money tied to the future of one company. The only way they could really diversify was for Jim to quit or retire from Enron.

Initially, Jim decided to quit but then reconsidered. Since he was relatively young, he wasn't ready for a traditional retirement. He enjoyed his job and had always felt that his Enron holdings had performed better than the overall stock market. Unfortunately, Jim and Melissa made several key mistakes. The first one, which isn't that obvious, is that the couple had no vision for their future; they hadn't planned for a "new" life after his career at Enron. Since he hadn't taken the time to create this new life, it was easier to remain in the comfort zone of his current work life. Secondly, Jim was guilty of what I refer to as rearview mirror investing. He assumed that the past performance would continue into the future. This is actually a common mistake but one you

stock. History has proven that sooner or later every company falls from the favor of the markets. Therefore, you need to change your approach: If you're fiercely loyal and want to hold stock in one company, these holdings need to be only a relatively small percentage of your overall portfolio. The bulk of your investments—the money that you're counting on for retirement—should be diversified, across a variety of investments that are in keeping with your investment strategy. Once you've secured your really important financial goals with this strategy, then you can "play" with the rest of your money chasing individual stocks or companies.

should avoid. No matter how well run a company appears to be or how experienced management is, any company can fall out of favor with the market and investors during various market cycles. This is why many investors moved away from well established but dull companies during the tech boom. Some of the upstart high-tech companies seemed to be generating much higher profits—but this didn't last. Investors with a smart strategy knew that putting all their holdings into the newest "company of the month" was risking their money.

MANAGE YOUR MONEY FOR A MARATHON, NOT A 100-YARD DASH

Two of the most popular races during the Summer Olympics are the marathon and 100-yard dash. In fact, it's very unusual for competitors to excel in each race. The man or woman who wins the 100-yard dash never wins the marathon. The training, conditioning and race strategy are totally different for the person competing in a 100-yard dash compared to the contestants in a marathon. So what does running have to do with managing your money?

LIFE IS A MARATHON, NOT A 100-YARD DASH

If you look at your life span, it more closely resembles a marathon not a 100-yard dash. Keeping this view in mind, you should aim for an investment strategy that allows you to accomplish everything that is important to you. You want to figure out what approach will enable you to get the returns you need with the least risk. If you're uneasy about this concept, you're in good company. Some people do have a strategy for winning a 100-yard dash. That's because the easy access to financial news 24/7 has prompted more and more investors to focus on the short term. Much of what you see and hear about is aimed at making a quick profit often from day trading and market timing—which is especially dodgy for most investors.

You need to focus on the marathon. What are your long term goals? What rate of return on your investments would you need to accomplish them? If you can comfortably answer these questions, then you should be able to describe your investment strategy (or have a financial advisor who can) and design it to *expose you to the lowest level of risk possible*. Here's what I'm talking about.

Suppose you had $100,000 to invest in one of two mutual funds or stocks that we'll call the red stock and the green stock. They both have a 3-year average annual return of 10% with yearly returns as follows:

RED	+40%-30%+20%
GREEN	+10%+10%+10%

Which investment account will be worth more at the end of three years? The green fund is the winner because it generated a consistent return of 10% each year.

The key to investment success is consistent returns over time. This is easier said then done. Let's face it, two out of three years you look stupid for putting money into the green fund. In year one, everyone else in the red fund is making 40% returns while you're only earning returns of 10%. In year three, everyone else is earning 20% returns while you're still only getting 10% returns. You looked smart in only one year. However, there's an important lesson here. You want to:

✓ Keep losses to a minimum

✓ Place greater value on consistent returns over time.

Keep these principles in mind the next time you hear a friend touting the latest hot stock or you read about some new investment idea. Remember, true financial success means that you have an ongoing stream of income that you never outlive, no matter how long you live and regardless of the rate of inflation.

Here's what happened with one of my clients. Some years ago, a young man moved overseas because of a job transfer. Shortly after he moved, he would send us a panicked email whenever his monthly investment statement showed a drop in value. He wondered whether we should be shifting his money around or getting out of the market. He was just very uneasy and concerned about the immediate future. Fortunately, the client returned to the States two or three times a year and came to see me. The preceding month hadn't been a good time for the financial markets and his statement was showing a decline from the prior month. At the start of our meeting, I showed him two numbers— the first his starting account balance and, the second, his account balance as of the end of the most recent month. He could clearly see that his account had increased in value, despite the losses during the prior month. The client finally understood the importance of a long-term view and he said that he no longer wanted to see monthly statements but would prefer to see just a year end statement. We both laughed and I explained that the investment companies and brokerage firms were legally obligated to send monthly statements to their customers. But I also reminded him that he didn't have to read them! The client was tremendously relieved and realized how insignificant

Sometimes I use the analogy of baking a cake when it comes to investments. You mix up the ingredients, and slide it into the oven. What happens if you pull the mixture out too early? You end up with a glob of inedible dough. But if you leave the batter in the oven long enough to cook properly, you end up with a tasty treat. Often, investors eager to check the progress on their cake end up taking it out of the oven too soon and too often, ruining any chance for a scrumptious dessert.

the monthly changes in his account values were when compared to the overall performance of his portfolio over time.

One month, I noticed that my son, Adam, had not added to his long-term investment account. When I asked him why, he comment-ed that he didn't want to lose any more money! I was surprised because I knew the year-to-date performance on the account had already been around 10%. But, Adam was only looking at his latest monthly state-ment, which in fact showed a decline in value compared to the prior month. When I showed him his account balance from when he first opened the account to the current total, he was quite pleased! Since he likes to surf, I asked him what he would think if a surfboard that nor-mally sold for $500 could be purchased at that time for $150. With-out hesitation, he instinctively knew it would be to his advantage to buy that surfboard, as the quality had not changed one bit. In fact, he would even think about buying three surfboards, so that he could sell two of them and use the profits to pay for the third surfboard. Since then, he hasn't missed a month of contribution to his long-term invest-ment account.

Note: To get more information on this and other financial topics, sign up for our Monthly Newsletter at www.BrianFricke.com. Free to readers of this book!

THE RIGHT WAY TO MEASURE INVESTMENT PERFORMANCE

Can you tell me how your investment portfolio performed last year? Don't worry—this isn't a trick question. Some of you will probably answer that your holdings were up X% from the previous year or that you outperformed the stock market. That is one way to assess your investment success but, in my view, it's not the right way.

As you've probably gathered by now—and you'll learn throughout this book—I'm a firm believer that you should be spending your time doing what you truly want to do. And, even though I'm a Certified Financial Planner (CFP), I know that most of you don't want to spend hours reviewing stock tables or figuring out whether it's time to reallocate your portfolio holdings.

Instead of focusing on your "Return on Investment," you should conduct a "Return on Life" or "WealthCare" assessment. Most people don't come *close* to living a full life. They are, in fact, *squandering* the astonishing opportunity that's been given to them. Your WealthCare assessment is a much better way to help you see if you are following your chosen path to living a full life, now and into the future.

THE TIMING YOU CAN'T CONTROL

There's no surefire method to "beat" Wall Street, despite what some so called experts may say. If that were the case, we'd all be lined up outside their door! The financial markets in this country have had dramatic swings over the past few years. If you were counting on a guaranteed return over time, you may have been disappointed, or worse, dramatically impacted if the losses in your portfolio were significant.

Since you cannot control the timing of either the market or your returns, you have to have an overall strategy to make the most of your life. You cannot count on guaranteed investment returns over an extended period of time. That said, there's a valuable financial tool—Monte Carlo Simulation—that takes into account timing risk and helps you plan for it. This tool shows you that your holdings depend on not just returns, but also the order in which you receive them and whether you're adding to your portfolio and when you're withdrawing from it.

Before you look at the charts that show the impact of timing risk, here is an example that proves how the same return each year—with different timing—has a dramatic impact on the size of your portfolio.

EXAMPLE: HARRY

Harry is age 54 and has $800,000 in his portfolio. He saves $16,000 each year. He plans on retiring in ten years and wants to have $100,000 available to him each year once he's retired. His portfolio is split 60/40 between stocks and bonds. Assuming a return of 8.43%, his estate will be worth $3.1 million when he reaches age 92. This sounds good until you consider the following:

Market Reality:

Real market at 8.5% (1954-1994):	Broke at 87!
Real market at 9.8% (1960-1998):	Broke at 90!
Real market at 7.5% (1940-1978):	$2.5 Million Estate

Would Harry prefer the higher return of 9.8% and run out of money or would he prefer the 7.5% return that would leave $2.5 million in his portfolio?

Taking Money From Investments

TIMING RISK EXAMPLE

$ 100,000	Starting Value
$ (15,000)	Annual Withdrawals

	Return Series #1		Return Series #2		Return Series #3	
		Year End Value		Year End Value		Year End Value
Starting Value		$ 100,000		$ 100,000		$ 100,000
Year 1	35.0%	$ 120,000	-10.0%	$ 75,000	11.6%	$ 96,574
Year 2	30.0%	$ 141,000	-5.0%	$ 56,250	11.6%	$ 92,751
Year 3	25.0%	$ 161,250	0.0%	$ 41,250	11.6%	$ 88,485
Year 4	20.0%	$ 178,500	5.0%	$ 28,313	11.6%	$ 83,726
Year 5	15.0%	$ 190,275	10.0%	$ 16,144	11.6%	$ 78,416
Year 6	10.0%	$ 194,308	15.0%	$ 3,565	11.6%	$ 72,492
Year 7	5.0%	$ 189,018	20.0%	$ (10,722)	11.6%	$ 65,882
Year 8	0.0%	$ 174,018	25.0%	$ (25,722)	11.6%	$ 58,507
Year 9	-5.0%	$ 150,317	30.0%	$ (40,722)	11.6%	$ 50,278
Year 10	-10.0%	$ 120,285	35.0%	$ (55,722)	11.6%	$ 41,097
Compound Return		11.6%		11.6%		11.6%
Average Return		12.5%		12.5%		11.6%
Standard Deviation		15.1%		15.1%		0.0%

FINANCIAL PLANNING SOFTWARE AND WHY MOST OF THE PROGRAMS ARE DEAD WRONG!

If you or your financial advisor uses financial planning software to help manage your portfolio, you're almost guaranteed to fail. Let me explain. These programs seem logical. You plug in the amount of money you have now, how much you're saving, when you want to retire, how much you expect you will spend in retirement, etc. The program then makes its calculations, based on an assumed life expectancy and an assumed average annual return.

This is the inherent problem with these software programs. The notion of a guaranteed average annual return over a number of years is simply foolish, even assuming a relatively conservative average annual return of 8%. About the only thing I can guarantee is that you'll never make an exact 10% return year in and year out. Some years, you will earn money and in other years you'll lose money. Rarely will you ever have an exact 10% return!

From my more than twenty years working with clients, I can say with absolute certainty that they are always spending dollars, not percentage returns. It's understandable you would assume that a higher average return will produce more dollars. HOWEVER, THIS IS NOT ALWAYS TRUE!

To clearly show my point, look at the chart below. It shows two different accounts. One account has a 5% average annual return and the other has a 10% average annual return. The same amount of money is withdrawn from each account every year. It would seem logical that the 10% average annual return account would be the better account. However, this is not the case!

Year	Return in %	Return in $	Contribution (Withdrawal)	Portfolio Value
				$100
1	0%	$0	-$7	$93
2	24%	$22	-$7	$108
3	19%	$21	-$7	$122
4	21%	$26	-$7	$140
5	8%	$11	-$7	$145
6	4%	$6	-$7	$144
7	2%	$3	-$7	$139
8	-4%	-$6	-$7	$127
9	-8%	-$10	-$7	$110
10	-12%	-$13	-$7	**$90**
	5%	Average		

Year	Return in %	Return in $	Contribution (Withdrawal)	Portfolio Value
				$100
1	-21%	-$21	-$7	$72
2	-9%	-$6	-$7	$59
3	-1%	-$1	-$7	$51
4	26%	$13	-$7	$57
5	14%	$8	-$7	$58
6	17%	$10	-$7	$61
7	22%	$13	-$7	$68
8	16%	$11	-$7	$71
9	13%	$9	-$7	$74
10	18%	$13	-$7	**$80**
	10%	Average		

As you can see, the account that only earned a 5% annualized return over the last ten years is actually worth more at the end of ten years!

How could this happen? The ending portfolio holdings are based on the *yearly return and when it occurred.* For this reason, the simple projections in nearly all planning software are not effective. Instead, you need a more complex tool that allows you to review many types of analysis that mix up the yearly returns, both the amount of the return (profit or loss) as well as the order in which they are received. This type of analysis will provide you with a more complete picture of whether your financial projections and goals are realistic, given the unpredictable and uncertain financial markets. The technical name for this type of analysis is Monte Carlo Simulation Analysis. You should find an advisor who is familiar with Monte Carlo tools.

WARNING

Your average annual return is not important. Don't focus on one number. The order in which you receive your returns is far more important. Since no one really knows what the future has in store, the best way to plan for an uncertain future is with Monte Carlo Simulation Analysis. Never make your financial decisions based on average annual return projections.

During the bear market of 2000-2002 one of our clients wanted to purchase a new boat. Naturally, they were concerned about the impact this purchase would have on their long-term financial future and success. Their initial thinking was to delay the purchase of the boat, until the market had recovered from its current downturn. After we ran the numbers through our Monte Carlo Simulation Analysis tool, we saw that their overall success rate would go down by less than 1% if they went ahead and purchased the boat at that time, rather than waiting for the market to recover.

Knowing that their long-term financial success would not be significantly changed, the couple chose to buy a new boat. I can only wonder how many hours of leisure and good times they would have missed if they had waited for the market to recover.

BEWARE THE SILENT MONSTER THAT CAN DEVOUR YOU

When my grandparents took early retirement at sixty-two, they did what pretty much what everyone of their era did. My grandfather had worked for the same company for more than thirty years while my grandmother stayed at home and raised the family. When my grandfather retired, they sold their home up north and moved to Florida. They put all of their savings into bank Certificate of Deposits (CDs). Initially, this strategy worked out quite nicely for them. Their pension and Social Security provided more than enough income to meet their everyday expenses. They didn't need the interest from the CDs so they reinvested their returns.

Then something funny gradually began happening. The pension and Social Security that had appeared so generous was no longer enough to support their lifestyle. Consequently, they began to spend the interest they earned on the bank CDs. This tactic covered their expenses—for a time—but eventually they found that they needed a new source of income to simply maintain their lifestyle. Like many of their peers, they had to decide whether to alter their lifestyle and activities or start spending some of their principal. Their choice—spending some of their savings—was not surprising. After all, who wants to feel as if they're stepping back? Why would you want to do less, having spent so many years looking forward to your retirement years?

This strategy was satisfactory for my grandfather. He and my grandmother still had money left in their bank accounts when he died at the age of eighty-seven. Unfortunately, my grandmother ran out of money and died virtually broke at age ninety-two. She was astonished at her situation, primarily because she had lived nearly twenty years longer than she had anticipated. Shortly before she passed away, she explained to me that she and my grandfather thought they would be lucky if they lived to age seventy-five. They had seen so many of their friends pass away. In an effort to keep their money as safe as possible, my grandparents watched themselves go broke, slowly but safely. They suffered because of their reliance on CDs. The downside to investments with a guaranteed return is that these returns won't keep up with inflation. You've undoubtedly heard the term inflation but it's a tough concept to understand because it is so vague. Unless you're unable to pay for some items that have risen dramatically in price, you don't feel the impact of inflation.

When I lecture, I often ask my audience to identify which attendee paid the lowest price for his or her first home. If the audience consists of people age 65 and older, it's not uncommon to find a winner who paid $10,000 or less for the first home. I then ask the winner whether he or she would believe me if I said—on the day he or she moved into the house—that they would end up paying three or four times what they paid for the house to buy a car. Usually, the person says something like, "You're an idiot. You must be crazy and there is no way I'd ever listen to your financial advice." Then, of course I'll ask the person what he or she paid for their last car. This is how you understand the dramatic effect of inflation!

HOW TO FIGHT INFLATION

What is your financial strategy to keep up with or out pace inflation? Thanks to modern medicine, you're going to live longer and you may need two or three times your current income in the future just to maintain your current lifestyle. I cannot stress this enough: If you need to have $70,000 annually to spend, you need to have a strategy to generate an income of $140,000 to $210,000 per year over the next fifteen to twenty-five years.

Don't think you'll live that long? That's what my grandmother thought. You have to assume that you're going to live longer than you think. If you think I'm crazy for suggesting that you need to double or triple your income, you're wrong again. After all, who would have thought that an automobile would cost three to four times what a starter home cost in the past!

Don't Trust The Government Inflation Rates

The government calls inflation rates the Consumer Price Index (CPI), which is supposed to measure the impact of inflation on everyone. Unfortunately, these statistics can be manipulated to some extent by adding or taking away items that make up the index. I can't prove it but I think the government manipulates the index to keep it low because the index is used to determine annual increases in Social Security benefits.

Know Your Personal Inflation Rate

The best way to avoid being eaten alive by the inflation rate monster is to know your personal inflation rate. You can do this by tracking your expenses from year to year. I've found this more effective than keeping a budget. If you're going to keep records of where you spend money, keep them so you can see how the lifestyle you lead is increasing in cost over time.

Don't feel too bad, however, if you haven't done this. Most people, including myself, haven't tracked expenses accurately enough to understand what our personal inflation rate is. If you're not going to keep careful track of your spending, assume a high, but still realistic inflation rate estimate. This will allow you or your financial advisor to do cash flow calculations to determine how long your money is going to last and whether or not you have enough savings to last for your lifetime.

FEES, FEES AND MORE FEES

If you're a smart consumer, you usually ask questions before you spend your money. For example, if you're hiring a decorator, you usually ask whether you're paying a flat fee, hourly rate or percentage of what you buy. You should know that you should ask—and understand—how your financial advisor is being paid. Some of my clients have asked why there seems to be so much variation in fees from planner to planner. The following letter is one I wrote to a client who was asking this question. In it, I explain why some advisors who claim they're not charging you anything may actually end up costing you quite a lot!

Dear George,

After I met with Pat, she asked me to write you to explain our fee schedule. She mentioned that you two have a friend who is invested through Fidelity who "doesn't pay anything!" She was wondering why you are paying a fee if your friend isn't.

Since I am always honest, I feel strongly about clearing the air. Everyone knows that there is no free lunch in life. No company is going to provide services for free. Your friend is paying although he just doesn't know how a percentage of his investment holdings are paying for the brokerage's fees.

If you can get a copy of his statement, I'd be glad to show you (and your friend) how much he's paying in fees.

I don't really expect you to ask your friend for his financial statements so let me show you the easy math of fees. A do-it-yourselfer using no-load mutual funds will typically pay 1.25% - 1.50% in fund fees and expenses each year. The investor doesn't see this charge as a dollar amount (since the fund companies aren't required to do so) but instead the share price is lower. You and Pat have Fidelity brokerage accounts worth about $786,000. If you apply 1.25% in fees, you would end up paying nearly $9,825 in fees every year! However, your fund fees are only about $3,930 annually the way we invest. In fact, you're saving $5,895 each year in expenses. If you deduct the money you're saving ($5,895) from our $10,000 yearly fee, your 'net' cost for our services is $4,105.

I would like you to think about your fee in the following way:

   ✓ *Could you recover this over the long-term if there was better investment performance compared to what you might obtain on your own?*

   ✓ *Will we save you this much or more in mistakes we might be able to keep you from making?*

   ✓ *Will you save at least the equivalent in time, energy, worry and recordkeeping?*

   ✓ *Some combination of the above?*

Naturally, I think you will. Otherwise my personal integrity would not allow me to continue our business relationship.

I have suggested to several clients that they read The Millionaire Mind *by Thomas Stanley. This book's thesis is that you have to think like a millionaire if you want to be one. Many millionaires credit their success to their advisors. I firmly believe that in ten or fifteen years from now, you will have had more satisfaction in your life because you have chosen to work with a trusted advisor like me compared to your friend.*

> *Regards,*
> *Brian Fricke, CFP*

PS—I'm sending you a copy of a book, Values Based Financial Planning. *Please read pages seventy-nine to eighty-eight. It should help you determine whether you are a do-it-yourselfer or a delegator. I only work with delegators. If you find you aren't a delegator, then we should stop working together because it will only add to frustration for both of us.*

THE SINGLE BIGGEST ISSUE IF YOU RETIRE BEFORE AGE SIXTY-FIVE

To help you understand health insurance issues if you're retiring before you reach age sixty-five, I've asked an expert to walk you through the choices you have. Tanya Burns, LUTC and RHU, is an employee benefit and health insurance expert. She has run Tanya L. Burns and Associates for nearly fifteen years and previously spent seventeen years as head of the employee benefit division of a local insurance agency. She's also a past President of The Central Florida Association of Health Underwriters.

In Burns' own words:

"Congratulations! You've worked hard, planned and saved and now you're able to do what very few people can: you are able to retire before you turn age 65. If you're in this group, the single biggest concern you have now is health insurance, unless of course you are retiring from a company that provides retiree health insurance. This option is unfortunately becoming less and less commonplace in corporate America. What do you do if you're retiring before age 65 and going on Medicare? Assuming your current employer has a health insurance plan in place and you are not working for a nonprofit, you will be eligible for COBRA. This is a federal law requiring all employers to make health coverage available to terminated employees including retirees for eighteen months after leaving your employer. The company can charge you no more than what their actual cost is plus another 2% to cover the administrative expense of providing the coverage to you.

"Often new retirees will gasp at the premium cost, especially if their employer had subsidized a large portion of the overall health insurance premium while they were working. However, retirees usually find that the COBRA premium is significantly less than what they would pay if they had to purchase individual coverage. If COBRA will be your only health insurance, make sure to sign up for it through your employer. Regardless of your health condition, your company must make this coverage available to you as well as any eligible family members.

"What happens at the end of eighteen months when COBRA ends? If you and your covered family members are healthy, you have two options. You can convert the COBRA coverage to an individual policy from the same company or carrier that provided your COBRA coverage. Your other option is to purchase an individual health insurance policy.

"In most cases, if everyone is healthy, it makes more sense to purchase an individual policy, especially if you can afford higher deductibles and are willing to use a healthcare savings account (HSA).

"What happens if you have existing health conditions or develop one while you are covered under COBRA? You'll need to be very diligent and make certain you submit the individual conversion paperwork to your carrier so your coverage continues without a gap. Depending on your condition or that of your family member, if you try to purchase an individual policy you may find that carriers will want to exclude you, charge you a higher rate or deny coverage.

"What happens when some family members are healthy and others have existing medical conditions? In these situations, it may make sense for the healthy family members to purchase an individual health insurance policy and leave the family members with existing health conditions on COBRA and convert their coverage to the individual plan offered when COBRA coverage expires.

"If you or a family member has preexisting health conditions, you work for a nonprofit, or you've never had any benefits, do you have any options? At this stage the only option available to you is the HIPAA (Health Insurance Portability and Accountability Act) guaranteed individual health coverage. You only have one plan to choose from and the rates can go up as much as 500% from the base rate depending on your condition. The good news is that coverage is guaranteed so you can't be turned down. However, because benefits are limited, the plan is closer to a high deductible health plan even though the stated deductible is $500.

While health insurance is costly, I cannot overestimate the importance

> **■ WARNING**
>
> **Sixty-three days is your magic number.**
>
> If you have gone uninsured for longer than sixty-three days—if you have retired and not elected COBRA or have chosen to remain uninsured—a preexisting condition waiting period can be imposed and you could be denied coverage under the HIPAA Guaranteed Issue program. The best is advice is DO NOT GO <u>UNINSURED</u> for longer than sixty-three days.

of having a health policy. I've seen a lifetime's worth of savings and investment portfolios of hundreds of thousands of dollars virtually wiped out by medical expenses in a very short period of time. Even treatments for non life-threatening health problems are quite costly. For example, the average hip replacement can cost nearly $30,000.

Do you know how much surgery and tests really cost?

Procedure	Range
Angiogram (diagnostic test)	$3,000 - $3,200
Angioplasty with drug excluding stints	$26,000 - $28,000
Valve replacement (coronary surgery)	$45,000 - $65,000
Cardiac bypass (heart surgery)	$20,000 - $24,000
Cataract removal per eye (eye surgery)	$2,600 - $3,000
Colonoscopy (diagnostic test)	$1,200 - $2,500
Hip replacement	$28,000 - $29,000
Knee replacement	$24,000 - $26,000
Brachytherapy (prostate cancer treatment)	$24,000 - $26,000
Radical mastectomy (breast cancer surgery) does not include reconstruction	$7,000 - $10,000

Source: Sovereign Claims Statistics - July 2007

"If you don't have retiree medical benefits available, you need the expert guidance of a specialist. You should look for someone who has made a career in the health insurance field. The person should have the RHU designation (Registered Health Underwriter)."

For more information, visit www.tanyalburns.com. Burns' email is tburns9@aol.com. Her firm's toll-free phone number is 1-866-722-8767.

DO YOU REALLY NEED LONG TERM CARE INSURANCE? A PERSONAL STORY

This chapter is an interview with Walt Ptashnik, a Long-Term Care Insurance specialist. I believe that Walt's experiences will resonate with many of you and his advice will help you make more informed decisions about long-term care insurance, now and in the future.

Q: Tell me your story. I know that you hate insurance in general. How did you become interested in long-term care insurance?

A: My 74-year-old dad developed stomach cancer in the 1980s. Before that, he had been very healthy so he lived for a long while with the disease. My mom spent everything on keeping him comfortable. I understand why she was willing to spend whatever she had to help Dad but the total amount astounded me. My parents had moved to the South to retire about a decade earlier and they didn't expect to have to worry about money. But, my dad's illness wrecked their savings. After about a year and a half, Dad passed on. Upon his death, Mom lost about half of her Social Security. Soon after, in the late 1990s, her investments took a hit like everyone else's. My mom was eighty-four years old and had to think about every dime that she spent.

Meanwhile, I was a traveling rep in the sporting goods business and my wife wanted me to get off the road and stop traveling so much, especially since I was frequently driving back and forth to Miami to check on Mom. Coincidentally, I met someone who was working in the long-term care insurance field. On some level, as a Baby Boomer, I understood how so many people would need this type of care. I also knew that I didn't want my wife to be in the same precarious position my Mom was in.

There's a simple reason why I have a passion for long-term care insurance. One of every two people is going to need care in their lifetime. That's a 50/50 chance of needing insurance. If you're going to buy one type of insurance, long-term care insurance is the type to buy. On the other hand, there's a one in 1,200 chance your house is going to burn down. That means you're paying a premium for coverage on an event that is far less likely to occur. It's a better deal for the insurance company. You do need auto insurance because, there's a one in 240 chance that you're going to get into an accident. But listen to these remarkable statistics: There's a one in twenty chance that you'll spend more than three days in a hospital as you age. There's a one out of two chance that you'll need long-term care at some point. You simply need this coverage—and the best time to buy a long term care policy is when you're young, not when you're old and your health is failing. Insurance companies don't want to insure people when the hurricane is coming down the street.

Q: Are there people who don't need long-term care insurance?
A: Yes, it isn't for everybody. For example, if you don't have many assets and little to protect, the premiums may be a hardship. You could prob-

ably spend your savings if you needed care and then get help from Medicaid. Long-term care insurance is useful for many, but not all people.

Q: Do you have any kind of a benchmark or asset guidelines for people to consider?

A: If a single person has assets less than $75,000, it starts to be questionable. If a married couple has assets worth less than $100,000, again it becomes questionable. There are also other considerations such as whether the couple has sizeable pensions, Social Security or an excellent income stream. In that case, you want to protect that income stream. On the other hand, some experts say that if you have, $2 or $3 million or more in assets, then long-term care insurance may be unnecessary. That's because these affluent people may prefer to self-insure. I have clients who have $5 million in assets who view long-term care insurance as a very minute percentage of their total assets that gives protection to a huge sum of their total assets. So, again, that would be the exception to the rule. I generally use a higher figure--—if my clients have assets of $3 million or more, then I'll start presenting self-insuring options. I'll give them a sense of what it costs to self-insure, not just at present but ten, twenty and thirty years into the future when they may need the care. Two or three million dollars may seem like a lot of money now, but depending on the growth rate of that two or three million dollars, there may not be enough funds to pay for the care of two people in twenty years.

Q: That's a good point. It depends on whether they're drawing an income off that $3 million or the money is just sitting there growing.

A: There are a lot of factors that come into play. There's no cookie cutter plan, although many organizations try to sell people on say, plan A or plan B. Choosing a plan this way means you're making a decision on the cost of the premium. Buying a policy simply because you can afford the premium isn't smart. You may be buying coverage that isn't going to protect you in the future. You need to find the policy that's right for your particular needs. Only you can evaluate these other factors. Someone selling you a standard policy won't know about other considerations such as charitable or estate considerations.

Q: Long-Term Care Insurance is now available online. Why should someone use an agent like yourself when the policies are available online?

A: The expertise of an agent can be invaluable. First, you always want to buy from an independent agent. He or she will let you review policies from different companies. On the other hand, if you're buying from a captive agent, he or she is working for one company. This means he or she has to believe the one product is the best. It may be the best for the agent but it may not be the best one for you. An independent agent will let you compare multiple rates and policies from many companies. I think that buying over the Internet isn't effective for long-term care policies. Choosing the right policy isn't easy. You have to consider more than just the cost of the premium but options such as whether to use a "return of premium" plan that will return all of your premium at the end of your life if you do not use them. Some return of premium plans will only give you back a percentage based on your age. It is important to carefully review the wording of the plan with an experienced and trusted independent agent. Other considerations include who the policy says can decide whether you need care. You want your doctor to determine that you're going to need care for a period of ninety days or more, or in insurance lingo, you cannot perform two or more of the activities of daily living. There are many plans that allow the insurance company's doctor or a doctor appointed by the insurance company to make this decision. You don't want one of these policies and it's easy to choose one in error. A reputable agent will help steer you clear of specific policies—even from reputable companies—with confusing wording like that. You also need to understand the deductibles also referred to as the elimination period could be "service days" or "calendar days." You want a calendar day deductible because that deductible of thirty days is really thirty days. With a service day deductible, if you only needed care twice a week, it would take more than thirty days to satisfy the deductible. These are just a few of the reasons why you should use an independent agent who specializes in long-term care insurance to find the best policy for you.

Q: How much insurance do you really need?

A: It's hard to give one broad answer. I want my clients to have enough, but not too much insurance. I show people the risks and then help them determine how much risk they want to take. For example, if care is $150 a day in a nursing home, someone might want to take risk and buy a policy that pays a part of that, say $100 or $120 a day. They will take the risk of paying the rest of that bill. Other people don't want to take on any risk and want the insurance company to pay everything. They're usually the people who choose low deductibles on their car, home and medical insurance. These people should look for a policy that pays everything or even pays a little bit more than everything to make sure they're fully covered.

This cost comparison can help you determine how much per day benefit amount you need.

Long term care insurance coverage is bought in dollars-per-day payout amounts, in ten dollar increments. You can purchase from $40 to $250 per day. That means when you are disabled, the company will reimburse you for the actual cost of care up to the benefit amount that you purchase. Any higher daily care charges must be paid for by you.

If the cost of care is currently $130/day, that doesn't exactly mean that you must insure for the entire $130/day amount. Here's why...

You have a dependable lifetime income from pension, social security, and/or investments that will stream in whether you are sick or well. Right now you allocate the income stream to support your entire retirement lifestyle (goodies, travel, entertainment, hobbies, etc.). When you are incapacitated, you'll no longer have to use your income to support that lifestyle, so now you can redirect it to help co-pay for needed care costs.

Example:

$50,000	Annual cost of care
-20,000	Your annual income
$30,000	Amount to insure for
$30,000 =	Approximately $80/day

So, if you are following the above example, you would only need to buy $80/day of Long- Term Care coverage, not $130. That saves you a lot of money.

Q: You've convinced me I need to work with an agent. How do I find a reputable one?

A: References. References. References. The 3R's. You want to find someone who specializes in long-term care insurance. Long-term care insurance is complex so you want a specialist. Don't just pick a name from the Yellow Pages. You need talk to friends, neighbors, relatives and financial advisors for their recommendations.

When you start talking with agents—and, again, I recommend independent agents—ask them about their experience, how they work, what fees they charge, the process and ask them for references. There's no reason why they shouldn't provide you with names of satisfied clients. Don't be bullied into making a quick decision by an aggressive agent. You should buy a policy when you're comfortable that you've selected the policy that best meets your needs. A good agent will put all the options on the table, not only the insurance options, but self-insuring, Medicaid coverage, family care, etc.

Q: When should I buy long-term care insurance?

A: The quick response is when you're young! Seriously, five years ago, I was working with people in their sixties and older. Today, most of my clients are Baby Boomers between ages fifty and sixty. Probably the ideal age at which to buy coverage is when you're fifty years old when the rates are quite reasonable

Q: Is there a minimum age requirement for this coverage?

A: Some policies set a limit of age twenty-five or twenty-nine but most policies require you to be at least twenty-one years old.

Q: Is there a maximum age?

A: Yes, most insurance companies will not cover people over eighty-two years of age. A few policies will cover people of this age but the cost of the premiums is usually prohibitive.

Q: Do the premiums spike when somebody turns sixty-five?

A: Generally the premiums do rise substantially at age sixty-five. The hikes may begin at eight or ten percent but then can go up to as much as 30% each year.

Q: How do these hikes compare to people buying policies when they're much younger?

A: Even in your fifties, you're going to have some acceleration in rates so you always want to purchase as early as you can if you decide that you want to buy coverage. The decision is known as "the cost of waiting." The longer you wait, the more it costs. Here's an example of someone who buys coverage at age fifty and ends up needing the coverage when he or she turns age eighty. The policy costs $1,000 a year so over thirty years, it would cost $30,000. The person might think about waiting to buy the policy when he or she turns age seventy so the person would only be paying the premium for ten years. But buying the policy at age seventy would mean the premium would be $7,000 to $10,000 a year. So over ten years, the premiums would cost a lot more than the $30,000 the person would have paid over thirty years. More importantly, the person would have had the coverage for thirty years, not just ten years. Remember, long-term care isn't just for health issues that are associated with the elderly such as strokes or Alzheimer's disease. In fact, 40% of all people receiving care are under age sixty-five. Many of these people have been injured in car or other types of accidents.

Here is contact Information for Walt —You can reach Walt at (407) 886-2023 or wptashnik@cfl.rr.com.

You can also get a special FREE report from Walt, Avoid the Three Biggest Mistakes in Buying Long-Term Care Insurance, *by calling his toll-free recorded hotline, 1-877-409-3500, 24/7, for a toll-free recorded message. I highly recommend you get his free report.*

LIFE INSURANCE IN RETIREMENT

Clients frequently ask whether they need life insurance since they're retired. I wish I could give an easy "yes" or "no" response but the answer varies, depending on your personal financial situation. These are the key reasons you have or buy life insurance when you're retired:

✓ To increase your pension income by 30%

✓ To provide a guaranteed inheritance

✓ To provide a significant charitable gift

✓ To (possibly) pay estate taxes

This strategy won't work for everyone, but when it does, it's fantastic. If you are entitled to a monthly retirement pension check, you'll have several choices on how you can collect your benefit. The two most common choices are single life (which gives you monthly income for life but payments stop at your death), and joint life (which provides you with a smaller monthly pension check but will continue as long as you or your spouse are living).

The chart below shows the options faced by one of our clients who recently retired.

Monthly Payout on Two Types of Pension Options

Pension Option	Pay Out
Life Only	$5,000 per month
Joint Life	$4,300 per month

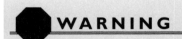

WARNING

This strategy won't work for everyone. You need to be aware of the following:

✓ You must be healthy enough to purchase additional insurance if this is necessary. I always recommend using term insurance with premiums guaranteed level for at least ten years. Policies are also available with premiums guaranteed level for fifteen, twenty or even thirty years.

✓ Use an immediate annuity purchased from a commercial insurance company to provide the income for your surviving spouse. Don't be tempted to invest in non-guaranteed investments such as stocks or mutual funds, even though the return potential might be higher. You're looking for guaranteed income here to replace the pension checks.

✓ Sometimes a spouse who does not receive company retirement benefits is also ineligible to continue company health insurance. Make sure you know your company's policy on this before choosing a life only pension.

The single life option would provide Jim with a monthly pension check of $5,000 for his entire lifetime, but upon his death, his wife Marge would receive nothing. The joint life pension option would give Jim a $4,300 monthly pension check ($700 less) but if Marge outlives him, she would continue receiving monthly pension checks of $4,300.

As you might imagine, most couples end up choosing the joint life (also called joint and survivor) pension option, sometimes to their detriment. In this example, Jim is giving up $700 per month or $8,400 annually in income in order to guarantee an income stream to Marge. This sounds like an insurance premium to me. The question then becomes whether there is a less expensive way to acquire enough insurance to guarantee Marge a $4,300 monthly check for a monthly premium cost that is less than $700, We checked with commercial annuity companies to see what single payment/deposit they would require in order to provide Marge with a $4,300 monthly annuity for the rest of her life no matter how long she lived. In this case, she would need $750,000.

✓ Federal or military employees are generally ineligible. These retirees often have pension plans that allow them to cancel the survivor benefit option, effectively returning them to the higher life only pension income.

✓ Before you choose the life only pension income option, make sure you consider these issues.

This is the amount of life insurance that Jim should have. He could buy this policy for $3,500 per year, which gives the couple an extra $4,900 per year in income! Over 20 years that's an extra $98,000 of income

If Marge outlives Jim, she has enough insurance money to purchase a lifetime annuity for her to maintain the same income stream. If, on the other hand, Jim outlives Marge, he is not stuck with a lower pension income. Instead, he will be receiving the maximum pension income possible. He could cancel the insurance policy or perhaps sell it using a life settlement strategy discussed on pages 76 - 77.

HOW ONE COUPLE TURNED $48,000 INTO A CHARITABLE GIFT OF $225,360

Don and Marilyn were in their seventies when they realized they had more than enough money to last for the rest of their lives even if some curveballs were thrown their way. In fact, they found themselves forced to make withdrawals from their IRA accounts even though they didn't need the money. Also, they had already made provisions to leave sizeable inheritances to their children so they didn't need to keep money for their heirs.

For the last twelve years, Don and Marilyn have taken their IRA distributions (less taxes) and applied it to two different insurance policies. The first policy they purchased was a joint life second-to-die type policy, meaning the insurance death benefit of $128,123 would be payable to one of their favorite charities after they both had passed away. They paid premiums of $4,000 for six years. At that time, we analyzed the policy and found there was sufficient cash value even on a guaranteed basis to maintain the policy. They decided to stop making additional premium payments to this policy. Instead, they decided to purchase another second-to-die insurance policy, this time for $102,237 payable to another favorite charity. They would make premium payments on this policy for six years. This policy has now accumulated enough cash to pay future insurance costs so they decided to stop making additional premium payments on this policy as well. That's how a total "investment" of $48,000 has helped benefit two of their favorite charities to the tune of $225,360!

HOW MUCH MONEY SHOULD YOU LEAVE TO YOUR CHILDREN?

When I meet with clients, I ask this question and usually hear that they plan to split their estate evenly among all their children. However, I believe this isn't an effective estate planning strategy. Effective estate planning means you leave an appropriate inheritance for each family member (or friend). The amount should have a meaningful impact on the person's life but should not be so substantial that the person does nothing meaningful with their life. This approach may require you to reevaluate your current plan. If an appropriate inheritance for your children and other intended heirs is less than what you've already accumulated, you should think about what you could (and should) do with the surplus money. If the inheritance that is appropriate for your children is greater than what you currently have, the difference or shortfall can be made up with life insurance, possibly with a policy you already own or one that you can purchase.

This strategy also lets you comfortably spend your nest egg with a clear conscience. You won't feel guilty, knowing that you have made provisions for a guaranteed inheritance for your children regardless of what funds you spend or how the investment accounts you have perform now and into the future.

WHAT TYPE OF LIFE INSURANCE SHOULD YOU BUY?

There are several types of life insurance but the right policy is the one that meets your specific needs. When my father died suddenly of a heart attack at age of forty-two, he left behind my mother and two teenage boys, fourteen (my brother Mark) and sixteen (me). Dad had purchased a high quality $50,000 whole life insurance policy from a trusted friend and advisor from church. In fact, the insurance company is a church affiliated company with a 100-plus year history. Needless to say, this policy was woefully inadequate for our family. My mother should have had life insurance benefits coming to her of at least $1 million. This would have given her the option of continuing the family business or remaining a stay-at-home mom. Instead, my mother was forced to continue running the family business. Years later, I was shocked but somehow not surprised that for the same premium my dad was paying for that $50,000 whole life policy, he could have purchased well over $1 million of term life insurance. Why hadn't the agent, our family's trusted advisor, made him aware of this?

I'd like to think the agent, was honest and well intentioned. But perhaps he was poorly trained or not informed about other policies. Still, I can't help but wonder how many thousands other families were put in a similar situation. Think about this—spend the same premium dollars,

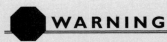

WARNING

Read this before you cancel or cash in any life insurance policies.

What would you do if you had a $6 million term life insurance policy that you no longer needed and didn't want to pay the premium? You probably would have cancelled the policy and stopped making premium payments. Unfortunately, if you did this, you wouldn't get any money back on your term policy. However, you could have sold the policy for $1.28 million!

There is a growing, but well-established business in life settlements, where institutional investors and companies will purchase life insurance policies that are no longer needed or wanted. These companies are often willing to pay more for policies than the cash surrender value of the insurance. In fact, the purchasers don't even care what kind of life insurance they're buying. They will buy whole life, term, universal life, etc. So if you know someone who has a life insurance policy he or she no longer needs or wants, have him or her look into a life settlement before they cancel or surrender the policy. It's not uncommon to get 300 to 500% more from a life settlement compared to the policy's cash surrender value. This applies even to term insurance where there is no cash surrender value. It's possible to sell the policy for 10 to 30% of the insurance amount. The $6 million term policy I mentioned is a real-life example.

There are certain guidelines for the policies that are bought. Generally, they must be at least two years old, the put the insurance company at risk for a $50,000 claim or for the same premium dollar, put the insurance company on the hook for a $1 million-plus claim. Which is a better deal for the insurance company? Why didn't the agent know any better? Maybe it was his training, maybe it was the compensation system the industry supported then and still does. The typical life insurance agent gets paid a percentage of the first-year premium. This percentage varies according to the type of insurance policy – term, whole life, universal life, etc. As I began learning about financial planning, I found out that the agent's commission on a typical whole life policy is anywhere from 100% to 150% of the first-year premium compared to a commission of 25-50% of the first-year premium for a term policy. The odds are unfortunately stacked against you. The insurers make their policies so complex that even the agents have trouble understanding them. Furthermore, there are incentives for the agents to sell you policies that pay higher commissions even if you don't need those policies.

In spite of these negatives, I still believe that life insurance is valuable. I own policies worth several million dollars. But, the type of policy that almost everyone should get is a term policy. Term insurance does get more costly as you get older and depending on your age, you may want to get a cash value policy instead. If you are considering buying a cash value policy or trading in your current policy, you should only look at low or no-load policies. With these policies, there is no agent commission. Instead, you pay a fee for the agent's assistance. As you might imagine, this type of policy isn't too popular with most agents but it is gaining wider acceptance in the investment advisor and financial planning community.

If you can't find such a policy on your own by Googling "no-load life insurance," seek out an advisor who is willing to use a no-load policy. Be prepared to pay the planner a fee but it will

insured must be sixty years or older and the insurance amount should be at least $50,000, although most prefer policies of $100,000 or more.

Be careful when selling your life insurance policy to a life settlement company. You are usually better off using an independent broker who can solicit purchase offers from multiple buyers. You also want to make sure and work only with brokers/companies that represent policy owners, not the investors. They should also be willing to disclose all fees and expenses associated with the transaction.

You will have to pay taxes if you sell your life insurance. You will pay zero tax on your "basis." This usually represents the lifetime premiums you've paid into the policy. Then you will pay ordinary income tax on any monies received that exceed your basis, up to the policy cash surrender value. Any money you receive that exceeds your policy cash surrender value would be taxed as a long-term capital gain.

be far less than the commission a traditional insurance agent would have collected. And don't believe that the insurance company pays the commission. Essentially, you're paying because the policy either has higher premiums or lower cash values or some combination of the two to allow the insurer to pay the agent commission from your premium dollars. At the end of the day, like it or not, you are paying. You now have the option and choice of deciding whether that fee or commission is fully disclosed to you in advance or if you prefer to have it kept a secret, shared between only the agent and the insurance company.

TAX ISSUES

You've all heard that old saying that you can't avoid death and taxes. Unfortunately, this adage is true and since I believe you should spend as much of your time as possible doing only what brings you immense joy and satisfaction, I doubt that filling out your tax return is one of these activities! That's why I urge you to use a tax professional to prepare your taxes—and let that person—who probably enjoys taxes a lot more than you—take care of this necessary evil.

To help you understand tax returns and some of the more common mistakes people make on their taxes, I asked Mary Guest, EA (Enrolled Agent), for her advice on this subject. In her own words;

"The single biggest mistake most people make when they prepare their own tax return is inverting their numbers. This includes copying down a wrong number or putting a number in the wrong box on the tax return. And I should know since for the last twenty years, I've prepared over 1,200 individual tax returns annually!

"Actually, you may be able to do your own return if you're only using schedule A and B (itemized deductions and interest/dividends) and generally don't invert numbers or put them on the wrong line. Most people get lost when it comes to filling out schedule C (self employed business) and schedule D (capital gains and losses).

"If you are tempted to use a software program to do your own taxes, don't assume that this solution will enable you to complete your return effortlessly. Right before last year's filing deadline, Brian got a frantic call from a client who had decided to do his own taxes. The client was a little distraught and even angry with Brian, thinking he owed an extra $15,000 in taxes due to a capital gain on a mutual fund Brian had suggested the client sell. The client remembered what he originally invested in the mutual fund and also knew what he sold it for. This was the information he entered in the tax return software program. However, the client forgot—and the software program didn't ask for—the dividend and capital gain distributions he paid tax on for the years he owned it. In fact, after the client contacted the fund company, it turned out his taxable profit was only $500!

"Who qualifies as an expert in tax preparation? There are three categories of professionals who prepare income taxes: accountants, enrolled agents and CPAs.

An accountant may have an education or background in accounting and may also take some tax courses. Accountants are generally experienced at accounting and business tax returns. They can do individual tax returns but their primary focus is on tax issues for businesses. If you're audited, your accountant can come to the audit if he or she is a Certified Public Accountant (CPA). Enrolled Agents are focused on tax return preparation, not accounting. They can represent you if the IRS audits you.

CPAs can prepare personal tax returns but their primary interest is working with larger businesses, which have ongoing year round accounting and tax issues, including payroll, financial statements, etc. Most CPAs will complete personal tax returns as a courtesy for their business owner clients but given a choice, most would just as soon avoid preparing personal tax returns.

"For personal and small business tax returns, I recommend you find an Enrolled Agent. They are experienced in these matters and their fees will probably be significantly lower than those charged by most CPAs."

TAX RECORDS YOU CAN TOSS AFTER THREE YEARS

Many people are uncertain what records to keep and when to throw them out. I advise keeping all your receipts for four years. This includes any receipts that will document deductions you are claiming, W2s, 1099s, etc. After four years, you can destroy those receipts. That's because the statute of limitations for assessing additional taxes generally runs three years from the date you file your return. Once that period has expired, the IRS is legally prohibited from even asking you questions about those returns. Alas, you can't go after the IRS for additional refunds either.

There are some exceptions to this rule:

- ✓ If you under report your income by more than 25% on your return, the limitations period is six years.

- ✓ Claiming losses for worthless securities extends the limitation period to seven years.

- ✓ If you file a fraudulent return or no return at all, there is no statute of limitations.

Assuming you've filed on time, including extensions, and paid what you should, you only have to keep your records for three years. Don't even think about tossing checks, receipts, mileage logs or other documentation that substantiates the deductions you've claimed until the statute of limitations has run out. As I've explained, that's usually three years but to be safe, you should keep them for four years!

TAX RECORDS YOU *MAY* NEED TO KEEP LONGER

✓ Investment gains and losses. You may have bought a stock five, ten or even twenty years ago. Keep all those records for three years after you sell and file the return reporting the sale. (Beginning in 2008, brokerage firms will be required to report cost-basis information to the IRS and presumably to you as well. But until they do, you or your financial advisor have to keep the records. You'll also have to keep track of investments purchased before 2008. The new law only applies to investments purchased after 2007.)

✓ Home purchase and improvement expenses. These should be kept until you sell the home. If your profit is more than $250,000 ($500,000 on a joint return), or you don't qualify for the full profit exclusion, then you'll need those records for three years after you file the return showing the home sale. Thanks to a tax law change in 1997, most homeowners probably won't face this issue. But, especially with the bull market in real estate in the early 2000s, you may want to keep yours longer.

✓ Actual tax returns. The IRS has the right to audit returns for up to seven years so you should keep these returns for this time period.

ELECTRONIC FILING

If you haven't filed your return electronically by now, you will in the near future. Almost all of my clients filed electronically last year. The IRS wants more and more people to file electronically. The good news is, as your return is processed electronically, there are probably "fewer eyes looking at it." When filed electronically, your return is almost instantly verified for information contained on W2s and 1099s. When your return is filed electronically, the IRS sends a confirmation to you or to the person filing your return the next day. That's right—you won't have to wait in line at the post office for the postage paid return receipt forms.

LARGE TAX FILING COMPANIES

What about the national tax filing firms like Jackson Hewitt and H&R Block? Although I know many people have been satisfied with the service from these companies, I wouldn't recommend them. Most of their tax preparers are part-time/seasonal employees with limited training. If you choose to use one of these firms, demand to work only with someone in the firm who possesses the EA (enrolled agent) designation.

Mary Guest, EA can be reached at:
Vaughn and Co.
6443 Parson Brown Drive
Orlando, FL 32819
(407) 620-8532

Note: If you're sick and tired of our current tax system, like I am, I urge you to find out about (and support) The FairTax. Go to www.fairtax.org.

KNOW YOUR STOCK OPTIONS

Do you know someone with stock options or do you have any yourself? Once limited to the executives of the Fortune 500 companies, more and more rank and file employees of publicly traded companies are being given options as part of their compensation package.

Before we go any further, let's review some basic terminology that tends to get misunderstood all the time. Stock options are not part of employee stock purchase plans, sometimes referred to as ESPP's. This is a program where your employing company will allow you to purchase stock at a 15% discount via payroll deduction. Stock options, on the other hand, are granted by your employer. They give you the right to purchase a certain number of shares of stock at a pre-set price. You're not required to buy the stock but have the option to purchase the stock, hence the name stock options. If the stock skyrockets, you'll definitely want to exercise your option and buy stock at what is now a very low price. In return, you could sell at the current higher price.

WHAT FLAVOR DO YOU HAVE?

Stock options are stock options right? Just like ice cream is ice cream. Try telling that to Baskin Robbins which is proud of all of its thirty-one different flavors. There are two basic flavors of stock options—Non

Qualified and Qualified (sometimes called incentive stock options). Here are the differences between the types:

NON QUALIFIED STOCK OPTIONS

When you purchase/exercise Non Qualified stock options, your profit is taxed as ordinary income to you and will be reported on your W2 tax form issued by your employer. It doesn't matter whether you actually sell the stock or hold the stock for continued investment. If you choose to hold the stock, any future profits would be taxed as capital gains. Any losses (based upon your exercise price) would be reported as a tax loss when you actually sell the stock. Should you exercise your non-qualified options early or hold on to them as long as possible? Most tax advisors and other people would tell you to exercise early so that any future increase in the stock price would be taxable as a long term capital gain. In my opinion, this is a terrible move.

An Interest Free and Tax Free Loan

When your company gives you a stock option, you have essentially been given an interest free and tax free loan. Think about it, you get the use of the stock usually for up to ten years. You pay the company no interest nor does the loan show up on your tax return. Where most tax advisors and well-intentioned colleagues miss the boat is in time value of money. If you exercise a stock option early on, you'll have to part with some of your cash to buy the stock and pay tax on the accumulated paper profit. This is money you no longer have available to you to earn interest, grow and compound. This is often referred to as opportunity cost. If you did the calculations, assuming the same growth rate for the stock, whether you exercise early or later on, in almost every situation you're better off exercising later on. This, of course, assumes the stock price goes up over time. A common mistake is to get too attached to your company and its stock. It is very common to see someone to has worked with the same company for ten, twenty or thirty years, become very comfortable and confident thinking the stock will always go up in value.

I remember one conversation with a client who had stock option profits, at least on paper, worth over $1 million. Since they needed this money to secure their worry free retirement I suggested cashing in the stock options immediately so they would be able to lock in the worry free retirement, they had hoped for. Convinced that the company's stock price would at least hold its value, if not go up in the future, they decided not to sell his stock options until he retired. They were hoping to save a little on income taxes by cashing them in when they wouldn't also be paying taxes on his big salary. No amount of convincing and cajoling on my part could get him to change his mind. Soon after he retired, the share price of the company took a big drop in value, making all of his unexercised stock options worthless.

The moral to this story is to understand the impact your stock option profits have on your financial future. In the example, the options were a critical part of the clients' long-term financial future. I didn't see why they were willing to risk their financial future for the potential of profits in the future—for money they really didn't need. On the other hand if you already have enough money accumulated to provide for your worry free retirement without needing your stock option profits, then it is okay to let them ride for a little while. Even if they became totally worthless, the loss shouldn't have a significant impact on your future retirement. The best time to cash in your stock options is—it all depends on what your total financial picture looks like and what your goals, dreams and hopes are for the future.

QUALIFIED STOCK OPTIONS (I.E. INCENTIVE STOCK OPTIONS, ISO'S)

This flavor of stock option can be better then buying a winning lotto ticket. When you exercise your right to buy these shares, your paper profit is not taxable income to you unless and until you actually sell your shares. This gives you an opportunity to have your profits taxed as long-term capital gains instead of ordinary income. This could translate into a 30-50% tax savings depending on your tax bracket.

If you have ISO's, it's probably in your best interest to exercise early and hold. You need to be careful about how many shares you exercise. While the paper profit isn't taxed as ordinary income to you, it is subject to the alternative minimum tax, which you could unknowingly create for yourself, by exercising too many ISO's in any calendar year.

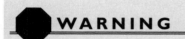**WARNING**

Incentive stock options are a highly complex area of the tax law. In many cases, your decision to exercise or cash out can result in a significant, unexpected financial hardship. **You could owe tax when you have received no cash income to pay it! Be absolutely certain that you or your advisor fully understand all the details surrounding incentive stock options. They're a very complex financial instrument, so you must understand the consequences of your decisions before you make any choices.**

Generally speaking, you should exercise as many ISO's possible every year without triggering the alternative minimum tax. If your company's share price tends to fluctuate, the best time is when the price is low. This strategy reduces your paper profit, which allows you to exercise more shares without triggering the alternative minimum tax.

PAY ZERO TAX ON YOUR ISO'S

You can, in fact, exercise your ISO's and not pay tax on anything. Exercise enough shares to keep under the AMT threshold. Hold them at least twelve months to qualify for long-term capital gain treatment, then transfer them to a tax-exempt trust (technically known as a CRT

– Charitable Remainder Trust). You're the trustee, you're the beneficiary and you can decide when and at what price the shares are actually sold for and how to reinvest the money. Again, you should check with your advisor as this strategy may not be appropriate for your particular circumstances.

THE ESTATE PLANNING PROCESS— A STEP BY STEP GUIDE

I have obviously helped many clients with their estate planning, as part of their overall financial planning. You'll see how I use insurance (this is not a disguised sales pitch for insurance! I do NOT sell any kind of insurance. But it can be a useful tool) to save clients money and protect their money for their heirs. Since estate planning is complex from a financial view as well as an emotionally charged subject for most people, I've sought another expert's help in explaining the process to you. I have worked closely with estate planning attorney Chuck Stark over the years in helping folks meet their estate planning goals. As a successful attorney he has helped thousands of families through this process. Here is great advice from a good friend of mine, Chuck Stark:

"No matter your age, the state of your health or the size of your portfolio, every adult has to address the problem of estate planning. There's no way to avoid it! You may think that you don't have enough money to worry about estate planning but if you're married or have children, you should worry about it. There are different ways to handle it—on your own, with attorneys, with other advisors, etc.

I wouldn't advise you try to do this yourself. You've probably seen the do-it-yourself kits or software. However, documents that you prepare yourself may not be legally valid. You may not be aware of this but upon your death, your survivors may pay the consequences.

The one choice that is the most sensible is to find a qualified estate planning attorney who will do quality work, listen to your concerns and charge a reasonable fee.

How To Pick An Estate Planning Attorney

There are several ways to choose an estate-planning attorney:

- ✓ Find someone in the Yellow Pages, TV commercials or other advertising

- ✓ Get a referral from a friend or family

- ✓ Get a referral from a financial planner, CPA, etc.

Once you've gotten some names, you should schedule a meeting. Usually, you can meet with the attorney for the first time at no charge. Assuming you are comfortable with the attorney and his or her experience, you should be prepared to discuss your particular situation. You should bring any documents that will help the attorney understand your particular circumstances. You need to do some homework before the meeting and think about your general plans for your estate. If you have children, you need to consider naming trustees. Think about how you want your financial matters handled should you become unable to handle them on your own.

Once the attorney has a sense of your needs, he or she should be able to tell you how much you will pay. The attorney may charge a flat fee or an hourly fee. Some attorneys will require a retainer before they do any additional work. The attorney can also explain the procedure. For example, will additional meetings be required to draft the documents or have you provided all the necessary information? Once you understand the process as well as the cost, then you will be able to hire the attorney—or talk to someone else.

Basic Estate Planning Issues

In order to understand what kinds of issues should be addressed by your estate-planning attorney, you should understand the primary goals of basic estate planning. These goals include:

1. To prepare for incapacity, which can occur as a result of senile dementia, Alzheimer's, Parkinson's, accidents, etc.

2. To ensure that your property passes to your intended beneficiaries at the appropriate time.

3. To avoid the court probate process.

4. To eliminate or at least minimize taxes (gift, estate and generation-skipping transfer taxes).

In order to prepare for incapacity, you should have a Durable Powers of Attorney which allows you to appoint a person or persons in advance of any incapacity to handle your financial matters, such as paying bills, filing your income tax returns, etc. Without a Durable Power of Attorney, you risk having to go to court for incapacity and guardianship proceedings—which can be time consuming, expensive and cumbersome. You'll also want to have a Designation of Health Care Surrogate, which appoints another person or persons to handle your health care decisions without going to court. Finally, you'll want to have a Living Will Declaration that expresses your intent in the event of a dire medical situation—such as when to prolong medical care and related issues

From a financial point of view, you want to make sure your assets ultimately pass to the people you want to have them—such as your son or daughter but not your daughter-in-law or son-in-law. If your children are minors, you will probably want to put your assets in trust for them until they reach age twenty-five or even older. These provisions can be put into your Last Will and Testament or Revocable Living Trust.

If you have a larger estate, make sure your attorney explains transfer taxes. These include estate taxes and generation-skipping transfer (GST) taxes. Currently, you're allowed to gift during your lifetime or at your death unlimited assets to a surviving spouse or qualified charity without incurring any transfer taxes. Usually, you can gift up to $12,000 (or $24,000 per couple) each calendar year to as many donees as you like. However, since laws may change, you should check with your attorney to make sure you are complying with both federal and state regulations on gifting.

You always want to avoid a court probate process. This can be lengthy process and ultimately your wishes may not be met. To avoid probate, you can do the following:

1. Give your assets away prior to death in which case the assets are not owned by you. (However, you would lose control of the property, which can have significant tax disadvantages.)

2. You can jointly own your property with right of survivorship. (Again, you are giving up control of the property and this can have costly income tax consequences for the surviving joint tenant.)

3. Name a designated death beneficiary other than your estate on your life insurance, IRA's, employer retirement plans, annuities, etc.

4. Properly drafting and transferring your assets to a Revocable Living Trust. You should ask your attorney how to avoid court probate for your individual circumstances.

Estate planning is necessary—not just to protect your assets—but to help yourself should you become incapacitated. Furthermore, the right estate planning can help save your heirs from very costly taxes if you use strategies such as setting up trusts, gifting money during your lifetime, naming trustees, etc. The first step is finding an experienced and reputable lawyer."

Chuck Stark graduated from the Miami University of Ohio with a degree in Accounting and Finance and received his Certified Public Accounting (CPA) designation from the State of Florida. He graduated from Wake Forest School of Law in 1986 and since then has practiced in Central Florida in the field of estate planning. His typical client has an estate from $1 million to $100 million. He can be reached at (407) 788-0250.

ESTATE PLANNING BASICS

Don't get alarmed when someone asks whether you've got an estate plan. This simply means a document that spells out how you want to transfer your assets upon your death. Obviously, thinking about the end of your life can be depressing, but I strongly believe that having an estate plan in place is an excellent way to maintain family harmony and help your children.

If you've done an effective job of teaching your children how to manage their money, save and invest and not accumulate a great deal of debt, then they should be capable of handling a very large amount of money without having their lives ruined. Assuming this is the case, there's no reason to place limits or restrictions on your children's inheritance. By doing so, you could create a roadblock that would prevent them from becoming the next Bill Gates.

On the other hand, if your children's ability to handle money is uncertain, or if they have special needs, drug or alcohol addictions, then it may make sense to put limitations on their access to their inheritance. You and your spouse should decide in your own words, in laymen's terms, what you would like to accomplish. Discuss this before you meet with an attorney. When you talk to your attorney, tell him or her in your own words what you want to do. They can tell what legal documents you'll need to accomplish what you want done, without causing undue confusion. If you are clear on what you want to specify in your estate plan, don't let the attorney confuse you with complex strategies or options that you're not interested in using.

Once you know what documents you'll need, ask the attorney what his or her fee will be. Ask whether the fee includes any retiling of assets that you are putting into a trust. Generally, it is best to agree on a fixed fee in advance for the work that will be done. You should also find out how the attorney does business. Ask about the process of reviewing and revising the documents. The worse thing an attorney can do is to create a set of draft documents and mail them to you with a note asking you to review them and call him. This is a huge waste of time. No one wakes up eager to review estate planning documents. A better approach is to schedule a follow-up meeting with your attorney. Have him explain each document or section within the document to you. Make notes of any changes or concerns you may have as you go along. By following this process, you should be able to have an estate plan in place within two weeks of your initial meeting with your estate attorney.

Don't forget, though, once you have legal documents in place, you will need to re-title your assets into the name of your trust. Your attorney and your financial advisor (if you have one) can do most of this work for you.

Like anything in life, without follow through you may as well not have even started. There are several stories that come to mind when I think about estate planning. Here's a few of the more interesting ones (names changed to protect confidentiality) so you can see for yourself the value of following through with your own estate planning.

AN UNEXPECTED WINDFALL

Several years ago, Roger called me because he and Nancy were worried about Nancy's father. He was in his early eighties and in poor health. The elderly man had very little money and Roger and Nancy didn't want the man's healthcare expenses becoming a liability for them, jeopardizing their own retirement. I assured Roger that their assets would not be at risk but suggested we meet to get a handle on all the details and facts concerning Nancy's father. We agreed to meet in about two weeks but Roger called a few days later to say that his father-in-law has passed away. Roger and Nancy finally came in to see me about two weeks after the funeral. As we began talking, I learned that Roger and Nancy were both sad and glad. Obviously, they were sad at the passing of Nancy's father but they were pleasantly surprised to learn that Nancy's father had left her over $1.5 million!

Nancy had always thought her father was in a tight financial situation. He always talked about having to pinch pennies and using old bread wrappers for garbage can liners, etc. Nancy, an only child, was astonished that her father had so much money but she was also sad that he never really enjoyed any of it for himself.

As the couple began the process of settling her father's estate, they found that he had set up a revocable living trust. Unfortunately, his entire estate still had to go through probate since he never got around to re-titling any of his assets into the name of his revocable trust, essentially rendering it worthless. Because her father never took any other estate planning steps, the first check Nancy wrote from her inheritance was to pay some $530,000 to the IRS. (At this time, the estate tax exemption was $600,000).

A FIVE MILLION DOLLAR INHERITANCE BLOWN!

Fred and Ethel, who were referred to us by their accountant, had all the outward appearances of success. Ethel was a tenured college professor and author of a book that was paying her royalties of nearly $70,000 every year. Fred owned his own marketing consulting company. Between the two of them, they had yearly income in excess of $300,000 and yet they had virtually no savings or investments. In fact, they didn't even have taxes withheld from any of their paychecks, instead relying on Ethel's book royalties to cover their tax liability every year. Some years, the royalty payment came before the tax filing deadline while other years it came after, causing them additional interest and penalties. For three years we attempted to work with them vainly trying to get them to withhold a more appropriate amount of taxes from their pay so that when Ethel's royalty check came in, they would have money to invest for their own retirement.

Both of them were in their early fifties so, time was definitely not on their side. We finally decided to terminate our relationship with them after three years when it was clear that they wouldn't act on even our simplest of recommendations. In hindsight, it seems that we cared more about their future than they did. The straw that broke the camel's back was when they told us they had just spent $40,000 on their daughter's wedding, all charged to a credit card. As they left my office for the last time, I asked them one last time why they weren't concerned about their future. Did they really intend to work their entire lives? Fred turned and said he hadn't told me everything about their situation. He then said that he was an only child and his father was quite ill. Fred's father had an estate in excess of $5 million, which is what the couple was counting on to fund their retirement.

About six years later, I got a call from Fred who was pleased that I remembered him. He wasn't calling for advice but to see whether I had any clients who would be interested in investing in an Internet start up (this was right before the technology bubble burst). He and his son had developed some technology that was going to revolutionize the way builders and architects worked together. Fred had already invested his entire $5 million inheritance in the venture, which was soon to run out of money. But he assured me great things were just around the corner. Of course, I politely declined the "opportunity" to get involved with his new business venture. We all know what happened to the Internet boom.

What do these stories have in common?

In both cases, the parents were very reluctant to discuss their financial situation with their children. Fred's parents allowed him to grow up into an adult with little or no financial training or education. Nancy's father did a good job in raising a financially responsible, independent daughter. His mistake was not being honest about his financial situation with her. If the parents and children had communicated honestly, I think it would have been better for both generations. Knowing Nancy as I do, I can't help but imagine her father would have had some life experiences that he never allowed himself. But thanks to his educating his daughter on how to make common sense financial decisions, today Roger and Nancy are living a "worry free" retirement way of life. They can spend months at a stretch traveling in their motor home whenever and wherever they please. Fred and Ethel on the other hand, are no doubt still working and spending and will never come close to experiencing the freedom and security of a "worry free retirement."

HIS, HERS AND OURS

Today, second marriages late in life are becoming more common. Many people want to find another companion after they lose a husband or wife. With these late in life marriages, it's not unusual for each person to want to keep his or her assets separate, primarily to protect the children from the first marriages.

The challenge then becomes how to maintain the relationship between your children and your new spouse without causing financial hardship. Unfortunately, if you leave everything to your new spouse, then your children have to wait for that person to pass away before getting their inheritance! I've seen this situation drive families apart. But who could blame you for wanting to take care of your new spouse as well as your children? The easiest way to solve this problem is to use life insurance. I'm not a life insurance agent and don't sell these policies but as a financial tool, I must recommend it in certain situations. Assuming you are insurable, you determine either the inheritance you want to leave your new spouse or children and do

Current tax laws are set to expire Jan 1, 2011. Under the current regulations, there is an unlimited stepped up tax basis on inherited assets. This may not be true after 2011 or if new tax laws are passed. Consult your tax and financial advisors before taking any action in this area.

so via the life insurance policy. Whoever doesn't get the life insurance gets your financial assets!

From a tax planning perspective, it's generally better for your children to be the beneficiary of a life insurance policy because a surviving spouse (under current tax law) has an unlimited marital estate tax exemption.

Remember, this is an overly simplistic view of how to solve the problem of what assets to leave to your second spouse and children from a prior marriage. There are many variations that you could use, depending on the complexity of your finances and your family. Regardless of who inherits your assets, you should take steps to insure that you make allowances for the stepped up tax basis on assets your heirs will inherit. If you bought a stock for $10 that your children inherit with a value of $100, they could turn around and sell that stock and pay zero tax on your $90 profit. If you and your spouse had bought that stock for $10, then her adjusted tax basis when she inherits your half interest would be $55, meaning if she were to sell the stock she would only have to pay tax on a $45 profit. (Your cost basis on 50% of original cost $10 = $5 + stepped up tax basis on 50% of spouses shares at current value $100 X 50% = $50.)

However, some surviving spouses unknowingly pay tax on the $90 profit used in this example. The IRS doesn't have to tell you how to minimize your taxes. You should consult an advisor who is experienced at handling the tax issues related to estate planning.

Here's another client story. George and Barbara seemed to have everything they needed to enjoy a worry-free retirement. Financially, they seemed set to be able to "do what they wanted, when they wanted and where they wanted. The couple had been married for over twenty years but they each had children from a prior marriage. Combined, their estate was worth around three million dollars, with one third coming from Barbara and the rest from George.

Their goal was to make sure that either person would be financially comfortable if he or she outlived the other spouse. But, they also didn't want to force their children to wait for their inheritance. George wanted to leave all the financial assets to Barbara for her to use and enjoy for the rest of her life, but at the same time he wanted to leave his children—but not Barbara's—a $2 million inheritance to share amongst themselves. The problem with this strategy is Barbara would not be able to continue her current lifestyle without having access to most, if not all, of George's assets.

The simple solution was for George to purchase $2 million of life insurance (with a low cost term policy) and name his children as beneficiaries. They would receive the inheritance George desired for them upon his death. They may also receive a "residual" inheritance upon Barbara's ultimate passing. We showed George how to use a special type of trust to own the life insurance policy, making the insurance money creditor proof—even from his children's creditors and/or divorcing spouses as well as keeping these monies out of George's taxable estate.

The couple chose not to purchase any life insurance on Barbara, because George felt that his assets alone would be adequate for his future financial needs, should he somehow outlive Barbara. Therefore, Barbara's estate documents and beneficiary designations were changed to leave her assets to her children upon her death, even if George ended up outliving her.

THE RIGHT TRUSTEE FOR YOUR TRUST

Designating trustees depends on how the assets of your estate will be distributed. If you're comfortable with your children and other heirs receiving their inheritance in a lump sum free of any restrictions, knowing they'll exhibit a certain level of common sense and good judgment, then the best trustee would be a friend or family member.

The trustee's job is simply to determine and inventory all the assets and distribute them according to the terms of your trust and/or will. The trustee could delegate this responsibility, which I highly recommend, to your attorney, financial advisor and perhaps accountant. Their involvement would then be primarily signing off on necessary paperwork.

If, on the other hand, you find it necessary to leave money in trust where it would then be distributed over a period of years or perhaps the lifetime of a potential beneficiary (a minor child, someone with special needs, or drug/alcohol issues), you don't want a friend or relative as the trustee. The family relationship is likely to become strained. So unless you don't care about the future relationship the trustee will have with your heirs, avoid naming a family member or friend if he or she will be in charge of distributing the trust funds.

Believe me, it's inevitable that at some point, the heir will pester the trustee to do something not in his or her best interest. The heir is unlikely to understand the trustee's responsibility is to act in a rational and responsible way.

In these cases, we recommend you find an independent corporate trustee, not someone from a bank trust department or brokerage firm owned trust company. You and your family deserve an independent corporate trustee whose primary role is to provide the legal, accounting and administrative functions of a trustee. Most bank and brokerage firms are happy to do this because they will also require you to use them for managing and investing the trust fund money. But, this is a major conflict of interest. That's why you and your heirs should retain the services of a competent "administrative" trustee and be free to change investment managers should their performance be shoddy. You lose this flexibility when you deal with most bank and brokerage firm trust departments.

If you have established a relationship with a truly unbiased independent financial advisor acting as a fiduciary for you, the advisor should have no trouble recommending several independent trust companies. The advisor could still manage your investment accounts, usually for significantly less than what you would pay a bank or brokerage firm trust department. The last time we surveyed these costs, we found we were able to do what most bank trust departments and brokerage company trust departments do with 30% lower fees. It certainly shouldn't cost more to have an independent unbiased trustee approach to your estate strategy and may well cost you far less.

DO IT YOURSELF WILLS SHOULD BE AVOIDED

Years ago I read about a businessman who wrote his own will, using forms purchased at an office supply store. After he died, the IRS said language in his will made his wife's share ineligible for a marital estate tax deduction. This led to unexpected estate taxes! It took several years (along with very hefty legal fees) for a court to straighten out the mess, overruling the IRS's objection and allowing the use of the marital estate tax deduction. The self-written will tied up his estate for ten years after his death.

Is this really a risk you want to take with your family? It always pays to have a competent attorney prepare these documents for you.

HOW TO PAY ZERO ESTATE TAXES

You have a taxable estate if you have assets exceeding $2 million dollars. If you're married and have properly funded trusts of $4 million dollars, the simplest way to pay zero estate taxes is to leave the taxable portion of your estate to charity. I'm very serious and encourage you not to dismiss this idea immediately. Consider the following:

✓ What is an appropriate inheritance for your children and/or other family or friends?

✓ Will it really require more than $2 million (or $4 million if you're married) to accomplish this?

If not, I encourage you to make arrangements in your beneficiary designations and estate documents to have any part of your estate subject to estate tax go to charity. You don't have to choose a charity. In fact, you can leave funds to your own family charitable fund. Technically, they are called donor advised funds. Here's how they work:

A **Donor Advised Fund** is a type of charitable giving program that allows you to get most of the benefits of your own family foundation without incurring the legal expenses or hassles of setting up your own foundation. They are often times marketed or promoted as Charitable Gift Funds. Most major mutual fund companies offer this type of program. Here's how it works—You make a contribution to your Donor Advised Fund and set up a *"Foundation Account"* that you name — such as, *"The Smith Family Fund"* — and claim an immediate tax deduction. You're eligible (assuming you itemize your tax deductions) to take an immediate tax deduction for each contribution. Because the Donor Advised Fund is an independent public charity, contributions usually qualify for larger tax deductions than those you'd get from setting up your own foundation!

You can donate appreciated stocks, mutual funds or real estate by contributing assets with unrealized long-term capital gains directly to your Donor Advised Fund. Instead of selling the assets and then donating the proceeds, you can give more to charity and claim even bigger tax savings.

Example: Donating Appreciated Assets

	Sell securities and donate proceeds to charity	Contribute securities to the Donor Advised Fund
With a direct donation to the Donor Advised Fund, you save an EXTRA $12,150 on your federal income taxes and your favorite charity(s) receive $9,000 more.		
Current fair market value of asset (Such as stocks, mutual funds or real estate)	$100,000	$100,000
Tax Paid* (15%) (Assumes a cost basis of $40,000, and long-term capital gains of $60,000)	$9,000	$0
Charitable Contribution/ Deduction**	$91,000	$100,000
Value of Charitable Deduction Less Capital Gain Taxes Paid* Assumes donor was in the 35% federal income tax bracket	$22,850	$35,000

Assumes all realized gains are subject to the maximum federal long-term capital gain tax rate of 15%. Does not take into account any state of local taxes, if any.

** *Availability of certain federal income tax deductions may depend on whether you itemize deductions. Charitable contributions of capital gain property held for more than one year are usually deductible at fair market value. Deductions for capital gain property held for one year or less are usually limited to cost basis.*

This is a hypothetical example for illustrative purposes only. State and local taxes, the federal alternative minimum-tax and limitations to itemized deductions applicable to taxpayers in higher-income brackets are not taken into account.

You "donate" the actual asset to your Donor Advised Fund instead of selling the assets and then donating the proceeds. Your Donor Advised Fund then sells the asset and invests the proceeds. You can recommend how funds are invested including recommending the use of your own investment advisor.

Your Donor Advised Fund can accept many types of assets such as cash, publicly traded stock, including control person, lock-up, and other restricted stock, mutual fund shares, publicly traded bonds, pre-IPO shares under certain circumstances and real estate.

Paperwork and Administration Is Very Simple

The "community foundation" that provides your Donor Advised Fund has already put all the legal documents in place. The foundation can also take care of all the tax and accounting paperwork required by the IRS. Your Donor Advised Fund verifies the IRS public charity status before sending your grant. Based on your specific recommendations, a cover letter is sent to each charity specifying the special purpose of the grant.

Recommend How Your Contributions Are Invested

You advise how the assets of your Donor Advised Fund are invested, including choosing your own investment advisor/manager.

Although the vast majority of grants recommended by donors are honored by the Donor Advised Fund, you should note that certain types are restricted by law.

Designate and Customize Your Grants

You (or your family members) recommend grants from your *Foundation Account* to the charities you wish to support. You have the option of being "recognized" or remaining anonymous.

Recognize

Your grant recommendation can be "acknowledged" to you, another person, or to the name you gave to the Foundation Account, such as The Smith Family Fund. You can even recommend that the grant be made anonymously, if you prefer.

Designate

You can recommend that the grant be used for a "special purpose," in memory or in honor of someone. The grant can be "restricted" so that it will go toward a specific use at the charity, such as a building campaign.

Schedule

Your grant recommendation can be set up as an ongoing remittance or "scheduled grant." This can be done monthly, quarterly, semi-annually or annually.

Build a Charitable Legacy

Whether your goal is to foster a family tradition of giving or to continue providing support to charities beyond your lifetime, your Donor Advised Fund lets you name both individuals and/or charitable organizations as "successors."

Individuals

By recommending one or more individual successors, you pass on your Foundation Account to someone, giving that person the privilege of recommending grants and the opportunity to make contributions. The successors can then pass your Foundation Account to the next generation, creating a never ending charitable legacy.

Charitable Organizations

You can recommend one or more of your favorite qualified charities as the successors to your Foundation Account. Upon your death, the designated organizations will receive the lump sum proceeds of the Foundation Account.

Note: To get more information on this and other financial topics, sign up for our monthly newsletter at www.brianfricke.com. Free to readers of this book!

SHOULD YOU PAY OFF YOUR MORTAGE?

 One of the best ways to lessen the stress of worrying about the economy or the direction of the stock market is to own your home debt free at or before retirement.

Many of you may be skeptical of this strategy because of all the hype about the value of the tax deductions related to owning a home as well as the notion that your money can earn higher returns than the interest rate on your mortgage. I can easily debunk both of these myths:

Lost Tax Deductions

For years I've offered a $10,000 reward to anyone who could explain how getting rid of a mortgage is going to cost me money. The popular but inaccurate argument is you'll pay more in income tax because of the lost interest deduction. The first person to give me a logical answer to this question—How do you make money when you give away $1 of interest to the mortgage company and receive back $.15 to $.35 (depending on your income tax bracket) from the IRS? —gets $10,000.

Anyone who maintains a mortgage to keep taxes lower is running this race in reverse. How long would you keep your money invested in a stock or a mutual fund if for every dollar invested all you got back was $0.15 to $0.35? If you're still not convinced, you should do some number crunching based on your situation. The chart on the next page gives you an example, which you can then modify to your own situation. Be sure to note on the chart the increased cash flow you'll receive from not having to make mortgage payments. This is the key factor everyone leaves out.

Here's a real life example: Ed and Elizabeth had a $320,000 mortgage with a 5.3% interest rate. They ended up paying off their mortgage. In addition to increasing their cash flow, they sleep better at night! This is huge. They're able to have less stress and fewer worries, especially during market downturns. If I divided my client base into two groups, those with mortgages on their homes and those without mortgages, guess who ends up sleeping better and not worrying as much?

Cash Flow Comparison—Mortgage vs. No Mortgage

	Mortgage	**No Mortgage**
Adjusted Gross Income	$150,000	$150,000
Tax Deductions		
Itemized	25,150	NO
Standard Deduction	NO	10,700
Exemptions (2)	6800	6800
Taxable Income	$118,050	$132,500
Tax*	22,360	26,093
Tax Increase with No Mortgage	N/A	3,733
Mortgage Interest (320,000 @ 5.3%)	17,000	0
Net Cash Flow (Tax + Mortgage Payments)	($39,360)	($29,826)
No Mortgage=$9,534 per year INCREASED cash flow, net after tax.		

*Example based on 2007 tax rates. AMT (alternative minimum tax) not factored into example

Earning Higher Returns than What My Mortgage Is Costing

You may ask why you should use investment capital that could be earning higher returns to pay off a lower interest rate mortgage. The mistaken logic here, of course, is that you'll be able to earn investment returns on a *guaranteed* basis that are higher than your mortgage interest rate. While the performance of stocks have been quite solid over the past decade, that's a short sighted view. You need to compare apples to apples. Here's what I mean. Your mortgage has a guaranteed interest rate you're committed to pay the bank. To compare investment return, you would need to find an investment vehicle that provides guaranteed returns at least 2% higher than the interest rate on your mortgage.

Most banks charge at least 2% higher for loans than the interest rates they're paying depositors (money marker accounts, CDs). Don't fool yourself. You're not improving your financial situation by keeping your money invested in other investments unless they are *guaranteed* investment accounts paying you at least 2% more than the interest rate you're paying on your mortgage.

While you find lots of stocks or mutual funds that have provided two or three times the return compared to mortgage interest rates, they don't guarantee these returns will continue now and into the future. If you insist on playing this game, be aware that you're *significantly increasing* your overall investment risk. However, if you're at or near retirement, you need to look for ways to reduce risk not increase it.

Here's a better investment strategy. Take the mortgage payments that you no longer have to make, once you've paid off your mortgage and invest those in your favorite stock or mutual fund.

Strive to Be Debt Free

The single biggest hurdle to overcome in building and keeping wealth is eliminating debt. If you no longer had to make your mortgage payments, credit card bills or car payments, you would have more freedom with your remaining investment funds because you won't need to get as high a return. Remember, lower investment returns aren't necessarily bad provided you're lowering your risk proportionately.

 **WARNING**

These comments only apply to non-retirement account investments. Pulling money out of retirement accounts to pay off debt can be done, but if you do it incorrectly, you could end up paying thousands of dollars in unnecessary taxes and penalties. Make sure you know the tax rules on retirement plan withdrawals or seek advice from an expert in this area before making a withdrawal from a retirement plan.

If you haven't done so already, one of your top goals should be to become totally debt free at or before retirement. If you have debt, get rid of it before you do any other investing. If you have investments and debt, sell your investments and get rid of your debts. Then take the increased cash flow you'll have and build back up your investment accounts.

HAPPILY DEBT FREE!

The single biggest obstacle to building and keeping wealth is debt. That's right—debt! If you're paying an increasing amount each month to pay off loans or credit cards, you are in good company. The average American carries an estimated $10,000 in credit card debt. Furthermore, at the end of 2007, late payments and defaults were up significantly according to card issuers.

Regardless of your circumstances, try to imagine having no credit card, car or mortgage payments. I bet you're seeing a pretty good picture! When you eliminate debt from your life, you reduce the amount of income you need to earn from your investments. This gives you increased freedom to be more conservative with your investment holdings, since you won't need to earn as high a return on your holdings. You'll be able to accomplish your goals but probably with less stress because you've invested in lower risk choices. If you're lowering your risk proportionately, then lower investment returns may well be acceptable to you. If lower returns come along with less stress and increased peace of mind, then this strategy may be the one you should be choosing.

People without debt worry less about their money. I say this with assurance, from first hand experience, having had conversations with more than 700 retirees! If you haven't done so already, one of your principal goals should be to become totally debt free at or before retirement. If you have debt, get rid of it before you do any other investing. If you have investments and debt, sell your investments to pay off your debts. Then take the added cash that you will have each month to build back up your investment accounts.

A REAL LIFE CAUTIONARY TALE

While I've known Vince and Noel for over seventeen years, we have only been working together for about three years. When we first started working together, Vince (who is in his forties) was employed by a technology company that had recently been purchased by a larger firm. As a result, his stock options became vested immediately and gave the couple a great deal of cash. They had more than enough money to pay off their mortgage but it took me over a year to finally convince them to do so!

Not too long after paying off their mortgage, Vince's company was bought out for the second time, by another firm. Unfortunately, this takeover turned out not to be a positive one for Vince and, in fact, he felt it necessary to resign even though he hadn't lined up another job. Still, he was comfortable making this decision because the couple not longer had a sizeable monthly mortgage payment. Fortunately, he was under no financial pressure to take the first job opportunity that came along. Instead, he has been able to pursue his next career option on his timetable.

I have the utmost respect and admiration for Vince. Most people, I think, would endure a difficult job, telling themselves that they'll make a change when they find a better opportunity—which may never happen. However, Vince intentionally put himself in a situation where he was forced to seek out a more appealing career opportunity. He was able to do so with minimal worries over his finances

I'm happy to say that as this book is being written, Vince is in the final stages of negotiating for a new position that offers him owner-ship potential in the future. This opportunity came about because the couple chose to become debt free.

HOW DEBT DESTROYED A FAMILY

In the early 1990s, one of our clients referred me to a friend. My client thought he was doing me a really big favor and, at the time, I thought so as well. I arranged to meet the couple, whom I'll call Tom and Mary. He was a senior executive with a Fortune 500 company and had been with this company for more than fifteen years. His income was over $300,000 (quite sizeable at the time) but he and Mary were very worried and apprehensive about their future.

They had nothing other then Tom's salary. That's right—Tom and Mary had virtually nothing other then Tom's nice income. They had the obvious signs of success including a lavish home in the right part of town but mortgaged to the hilt so they had, virtually no equity. They leased two cars, a Mercedes for Tom and a Jaguar for Mary. Their financial goals were clear: Tom wanted to be able to retire within five years. Susie, their daughter, was getting married in six months and they wanted to make a luxurious wedding for her. Their son, Tom Jr., would be starting college the next year and they naturally wanted to send him to the best college money could buy. They also had accumulated $80,000 of credit card debt and had no other savings or investments, except for Tom's modest 401(k) plan. He boasted that he had deposited $5,000 in this account over the previous five years (to me, that's a pretty paltry sum, given his salary).

From the couple's view, my job as their financial advisor was really quite simple. I was supposed to tell Tom and Mary what they needed to do to accomplish all their goals without sacrificing current lifestyle. Much to their dismay, I told them that I couldn't take them on as clients. The reason? I've always found it difficult, if not impossible to help someone who isn't willing to help himself. I did give the couple some free advice. I told them—spend less, save more and pray a lot.

Recently, I learned that Tom and Mary were divorced a few years ago. Apparently, Mary began to resent all the time her husband was spending at work. With the children grown and out of the house, she wanted to spend time with her husband in "retirement." Things were a bit more complicated. Tom lost his job, apparently because management had difficulty trusting him to run a multibillion-dollar operation when he couldn't keep his own personal finances straight. Also, the couple's children no longer "love" their parents who can't spoil— I mean help them out—the way they had in the past. The children have had to get jobs and support themselves.

You've probably seen the bumper sticker, which says, "I owe, I owe, so it's off to work I go." The choice is yours. You must take control of your money. If you don't, it will take control of you and your life and you're probably not going to be happy under its thumb.

GETTING THE BEST
MORTGAGE DEAL

Finding the best mortgage when you're buying a house is challenging. Not only are there many types of mortgages but many different ways to get them. To help you sort your way through the mortgage maze, Rod Harter, our mortgage expert we refer all our clients to, offers his advice on how to find the right mortgage for your particular needs.

In Harter's own words:

"Competition for mortgage loans is ferocious. In addition to a shrinking market, the Internet is complicating matters by equalizing the mortgage industry and making all loan officers look the same. All this additional information confuses buyers. In fact, nothing could be further from the truth. Most mortgage companies are content to offer the lowest price, complete the transaction and move on. However, a true mortgage professional works differently by taking the time to evaluate and recommend a mortgage strategy that best meets a homeowner's unique financial goal. I believe in integrating the mortgage into their personal financial plan. That's where I have the most pride and enjoyment working with my clients.

In the past, originators simply provided a loan transaction, but today as a professional mortgage representative I have to be more financially savvy than ever. I must be a better mortgage advisor to show my clients how to manage their mortgage dollar over time, not just quote the lowest payment. Inexperienced home buyers end up rate shopping, largely because they distrust the process and may believe the average loan officer who gives the lowest up-front rate or lowest cost is actually offering the best deal. With their guard up, their fears often prevent them from seeing the mortgage professional as a trusted advisor.

Some of my customers would probably rather get a root canal than spend a lot of time discussing their mortgage options with me. There are so many choices that it's like looking through a kaleidoscope for most borrowers. My clients tell me that they relish my services as an advisor. Here's what they say:

'We really see the value of paying more for your services. Your analysis and personal consultation showed us things we never gave thought to. It is amazing how much we learned by studying your reports and your recommended debt structure. I had no idea we were about to let $42,401.00 slip through our fingers over the next five years. I hate to think how much we could have saved over the last 20 years.

I know one thing for sure; we are not going to make this mistake again. Even our CPA was surprised with the report we provided him. He was not aware a local mortgage expert was available for these types of detailed reviews. He's currently meeting with us to figure out what to do with our additional cash. Thanks again for your advice and for always answering your telephone!' Robert & Cathy Golati, Orlando, FL

When working with a client, my goal is to quickly and easily show them the mortgage plan that is right for them. It has to fit like a good suit. The tools I use include reports offered by Mortgage Coach such as a Total Cost Analysis, Rent vs. Buy, RateWatch, Debt Consolidation Analysis and Equity Repositioning Analysis. These sophisticated mortgage analyzers transform me from a typical mortgage representative to a trusted advisor. Only 12% of people in the mortgage industry including big banks and mortgage companies use this software. When you take the time to place your numbers in our loan analyzer the results are rather surprising at times. Sometimes what I think is going to be a good scenario turns out to not look so attractive. We can include the tax benefits, the interest costs as well as many other factors.

Very often, when a potential new customer calls, they only want to know what mortgage has the lowest rate and cost. Rate shoppers focus the entire mortgage buying decision on the rate and loan fees. At this pivotal point, the potential borrower has no ties to me unless I quickly establish trust and respect.

Rate shopping goes on at all levels. With the help of the mortgage analysis tools I utilize, I am able to move the conversation to a higher level. You can come to me and say, 'What is your best 30-year fixed rate? I can answer, but then I ask, 'Why do you want a 30-year fixed? Have you thought about a 10/1 or a 5/1?' Then I can use Mortgage Coach to show the difference and show how that equates to the life of the loan. In addition, I can take the difference in that payment and show that if you put that monthly savings into an investment account, at the end of six, eight or 10 years, I can show how much you have gained.

'We should have listened to your advice the last time but we had a family relative that begged for our business. He was new in the business and had no idea how to analyze our loan scenario. We learned a big lesson. You came highly recommended but we felt pressure from our family. Only months after financing our previous home we learned from the reports you sent us that we were paying the highest possible premium on the money we borrowed. You taught us a valuable lesson and dare I say it was an expensive one. Well, we've since sold that house and now live in a home we hope to retire in.

Thanks for providing us all the extra advice and mortgage analysis to help us make the right decision. We have learned a lot about equity and having too much cash trapped in our home is not always the best use of our money. Your strategic financial plan and your mortgage analysis make it very easy for us to follow. I like your style of no smoke and mirrors, just smart financing with a short and long-term plan of execution. Thanks to you and Christina for waiting for us to come around.' Bob and Regina Weston, Windermere, FL

The fact that we can show that information and make it clear and precise is different than simply saying you're going to be saving $20 a month. The Mortgage Coach empowers me with the automation and systems to quickly and effectively deliver mortgage advice that changes the lives of my clients, rather than just quoting rates and fees with an average good faith estimate.

Rod Harter is America's Mortgage Expert. You can reach Rod at rharter1@cfl.rr.com or 407-599-6888x122. Be sure and ask for his FREE Report, "19 Secrets Banks & Mortgage Companies Hope You Never Find Out About."

THE BEST WAY TO BUY A CAR

By now, you know that I believe in spending time doing the things I enjoy doing. I'd rather seek professional help with activities that I dislike and I'm not expert at. That's why I'm especially pleased to offer you advice from Gary Leudeck, an experienced auto broker (Gary has nearly thirty years of experience in the car business and has done virtually every job in the business from repairs to sales). I have no hesitation recommending Gary's services to all my clients and anyone I meet.

Here's Gary's advice, in his own words:

"Many people don't realize they can employ the services of an automobile broker to purchase a late model or low mileage car, often at tremendous savings over what it would cost to buy a new car. This is what I do – I am an auto broker. I buy cars for my clients through auto auctions. And, I'm going to share the secrets the auto dealers hope you never find out!

Buying a new car can be very intimidating and as a result, most people purchase a new car with little or no preparation. Walking into a new car dealership can be a very scary experience if you don't know what you're doing. Dealers don't have the best reputation and like most businesses, it just takes a handful of dealers give the rest of the industry a black eye. Many of them have been known to play little tricks and gimmicks with buyers such as altering the invoice. Buying a big ticket item like a car is usually driven by emotion so when consumers think they've gotten a great deal, there is a greater chance they will move forward with their purchase. Dealers are experts at creating positive emotion, so they manipulate the numbers to make the buyer think they are negotiating a great deal for themselves.

Other times people have gone to dealers using their present car as a trade. Some dealers have actually sold the customer's car to an auto wholesaler *before* the customer even makes a final decision to move forward with a purchase of a new car. Make sure you give yourself ammunition before you buy a new car by doing some homework ahead of time. Check around on the Internet. You can get a good idea which dealers have a good and bad reputation. Call the Department of Motor Vehicles (DMV) and ask how many complaints a particular dealership has received. Registered complaints are kept on file. This kind of information will help determine if you're dealing with a reputable company. If you hear any complaints about a particular dealership, simply don't go there.

THE BEST TIME TO BUY

There are certain times of the month and specific months where you can get a great deal on a new car. It is always better to negotiate price at the end of the month. That's when dealers are aggressively trying to close out their month or make their sales quotas. You're always better off strolling into the dealership the last day of the month. Put your poker face on and have some fun in the process.

August and September are the best months to buy a new car because that's when the new models will be arriving. You'll be able to negotiate great deals on the car you want and you should also shop at the end of these months. You may also be able to take advantage of local dealer incentives or rebates.

LEASING

People are often confused about whether leasing is a good deal—in certain circumstances, it can be very advantageous. Here's my basic rule of thumb on leasing vs. financing. If you can finance a car and secure "zero" percent financing, your payments may be very close to the same payment as a lease. If that's the case, always buy the car rather than lease it. On the other hand, if you cannot afford to buy a car or you want to drive a particular make or model that is included in a leasing special, then you lease. But, never lease for more than two years.

The key disadvantage to leasing is that dealers make it very difficult for you to get out of one lease without entering another. You'll end up paying sizeable penalties to change the terms or the lease. Also, if you wreck a leased car, you still have to keep it through the full term of the original agreement.

Don't buy a car at the end of a lease. For a comparable price, I can usually find you the same car a year newer with half the miles on it.

For more information on Gary Luedeck and his services, check his website: www.auctionlocators.net, or phone him at his office 407-831-2002 or on his cell at 407-592-7245.

KIDS AND MONEY: DON'T BE YOUR CHILD'S OR GRANDCHILD'S ATM

"You can't build wealth buying things you don't need with money you don't have to impress people you don't care about." –Unknown

 Clients frequently ask for my advice about educating kids (or grandkids) about money. As a father of two teenage boys, my wife and I have developed a set of "money rules." I will share them with you:

Allowances

We started giving our boys allowances when they were five or six years old. We have paid them a weekly allowance equal to their age. A five-year-old would be paid five dollars weekly and a fifteen-year-old would be paid $15 weekly. They are not able to spend all this money. We require them to give away at least 10% of their income to charity. For us, this means church. Another 10% is set aside for long-term savings. The rest is available for spending, short-term saving for a purchase that costs more than one week's allowance, or adding to their long-term savings. They are not paid for doing specific chores. Instead, we expect them to be a contributing member of the family. Each family member has responsibilities appropriate for their age. We reserve the right to deduct money from their allowance when they don't keep up with chores and other responsibilities or if they make bad decisions. We pay for the basic necessities, but they are responsible for everything else. For us, this meant providing clothes of our choosing for school. If they wanted expensive designer jeans or Michael Jordan tennis shoes, they would be responsible for buying these items. They would also be responsible for paying for birthday and Christmas gifts.

For short-term savings we opened savings accounts at our bank. Since the boys are minors, we set them up as joint accounts, with their name on the account. We also had ATM cards issued to each of them so they could access money when they needed it. We also explained ATM fees so they wouldn't waste money on ATM withdrawal fees. When Justin turned seventeen, we opened a joint checking account with him. Most banks won't allow a minor on a checking account but you should try to find a bank that will. This provides another opportunity for a child to learn firsthand how to use, balance and keep track of his or her own checking account.

This strategy has turned into a wonderful learning tool to teach our children the value of money. When Adam was about eleven, he had picked out a $30 video game to buy for a friend's birthday. When his mother asked if he had brought his wallet along, suddenly, he was surprised that he would be paying for the video game! He quickly decided that his friend would appreciate a nice birthday card and a $10 gift certificate. My wife called his friend's mother to let her know what our money rules were, so the other family wouldn't think the more modest gift was a reflection on the value of their friendship. The birthday boy's family has now implemented similar rules for their family.

Cars

We don't advocate giving cars to children. They need to know that they have to earn and save for large purchases such as a car. My children know they can buy their own cars when they reach age eighteen.

The biggest gift you can give your children is to raise them to be independent, self sufficient, contributing members (as opposed to "takers") of society. We have chosen to purchase a "spare" family vehicle. I am very clear with the boys that I own it! It's my car that I am letting them borrow. This lets me restrict or take away access to the vehicle should I ever find it necessary. I will chip in on some gas money and in return, they

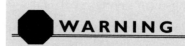

WARNING

I do know some families will buy a car for their children. In certain circumstances, this makes sense. If the child earns excellent grades and gets a full college scholarship, I would encourage parents to buy a car, provided the child has shown he or she is mature and responsible. Again, children should feel a sense of pride and accomplishment, knowing they "paid" for their own college education via their good grades. This is tangible evidence that they're becoming independent, self sufficient, and making a contribution to society.

are expected to run occasional errands for us. However, we don't pay for all their gas purchases; they pay for their gas when they're driving for their own personal use, visiting friends, going out on dates, etc. We also pay for their insurance, but we assume they will qualify for all of the good driver and good student discounts that are available. If they don't qualify for these discounts, they are responsible for paying the increased insurance premiums.

Shortly after my oldest son Justin turned sixteen, he got a speeding ticket. The fine was over $200 and Justin asked permission to withdraw money from his long-term savings account. (For long-term savings we use a uniform gift to minor account at a discount brokerage. Since I'm the custodian, Justin needs my permission to withdraw money from the account.) He was a little annoyed when I told him that he couldn't withdraw the money. Justin barely had enough funds in his checking and savings account to pay the fine. He wouldn't be able to do fun things like going to the movies for about a month. This was a wonderful opportunity to reinforce the concept of long-term savings. You don't take money out of long term savings for anything except your long-term savings goal. Poor decisions or irresponsible actions are not a good reason for touching your long-term savings. Sometimes experience is the best teacher!

Part-Time Jobs

Teens should be involved in some form of after school activity, such as sports or club or hobby. My sons know they are expected to have a part-time job after school if they don't have another after school activity. Some parents discourage their teenagers from working but I feel strongly that the earlier you can instill in a child the sense pride and accomplishment that comes from earning his or her money, the better off they will be!

Long-Term Savings

I prefer using UGMA (uniform gift to minor accounts) also known as UTMA (uniform transfer to minor accounts). A parent typically serves as custodian for the account, which uses the child's Social Security number for tax reporting purposes. I established discount brokerage accounts for both of the boys and have invested their long-term savings in no-load growth mutual funds. I make the investment decisions and give them copies of their monthly statements. On occasion, they have asked me about the account. This strategy makes more sense than trying to force feed them a financial education.

WARNING

It's important that you remember that a UGMA becomes your son or daughter's account when the child reaches age eighteen. For this reason, I closely monitor the amount of money in the account. I don't want the account to hold too much money in case the child ends up making a poor financial decision. I have conditioned my children to think of these accounts as the money they will use to purchase their first car.

College Savings Accounts

I haven't used 529 college savings plans or Roth IRA plans because I want my sons to understand enough about money and investing to make decisions about their college education. They will need to choose whether to spend money for a private institution vs. a state or community college. I don't believe in stashing money in a college account for young kids. I believe it's important your children learn the value of making choices—having some short-term rewards and setting aside money for future expenses.

401k Dad

To encourage my boys to save and invest more than the minimum 10% for long-term savings, I have promised them that I will match 100% what they spend for their first car purchase. This promise comes with two caveats—they must pay cash and purchase a used car. Let's face it, a teenager's first car is typically going to get some scratches and dents. I'd rather have that happen on reliable used car than a new one!

Buying Stocks for Kids/Grandkids

Every year, well meaning grandparents ask me how to buy stocks or another investment for their grandchildren. I'm just not a fan of this strategy! It's a parent's (not grandparent's) responsibility to teach their kids about money and finances. But, I do have some recommendations for other ways you can help your kids or grandkids:

- ✓ Send the child a check with the payee blank! Give them instructions to make the check payable to a worthy cause of their choosing! You fill in the dollar amount. They decide which charity gets it. While you run the risk that the child will make the check out to him or herself, this is likely to happen only once!

✓ Find out what the children saved from their allowance in long-term savings during the past year and match it! You don't have to match it 100%. You could match it with 25 or 50% of whatever they save on their own. This shows that good habits can be rewarded.

Grown Kids Returning Home

A number of our clients have firsthand experienced "boomerang" kids. This is when grown children move back home, perhaps because they don't have a job, have gotten divorced or need help with a health or other life crisis. Needless to say these living conditions can add a level of stress and discomfort to everyone involved. Don't let money issues add to it! If you find yourself in this situation, have a written agreement that spells out the financial expectations of each party. This document should discuss items such as utility bills, food, use of automobiles and household chores. In other words, specify who will be responsible for different chores and expenses. Having a written document will help you avoid any misunderstanding in the future. Defining responsibility may also provide added motivation for the child to return as quickly as possible to his or her own independent living.

Giving or Loaning Money to Kids

It's fairly common for parents to give money to their adult children. Sometimes, parents want to help their children make the down payment on a home or invest in a business. Other times, the adult child asks his or parents for help. I wouldn't tell you not to help your children, but, it's important you recognize that if you're making a gift, there shouldn't be any strings attached. You shouldn't make them feel indebted or obligated to you. On the other hand, you may feel more comfortable loaning the money to your children, spelling out in writing a repayment schedule. You are making a business transaction, just as if they had gone to a bank. You can of course forgive part, or the entire loan at some point in the future.

Several years after my wife and I had purchased our first home, we decided to put on a room edition. Instead of getting a loan from the bank, we borrowed the money from my mother. Given the relatively modest interest rates offered by banks on deposits, she actually made more money by loaning us the funds. We paid her 8%, compared to the 4% rate banks were offering on CDs. It was convenient for us, and a way for my mom to double her income on that money. I insisted on drawing up a loan agreement that spelled out that we would make regular monthly payments, and we eventually ended up paying off the loan ahead of time. Since we had a loan agreement, we didn't feel obligated to get "mom's approval" for any of the improvements.

Unfortunately, some people don't want to formalize loans in the family. It almost always ends badly. One of our clients loaned their son and daughter-in-law money to purchase a home. They had a verbal understanding that this loan would be repaid with interest. However, the son and daughter-in-law ended up getting divorced and selling the home. Because there was no loan agreement or legal document the now ex-daughter-in-law refused to accept any financial responsibility for repaying her share of this loan.

Involve Your Family in Your Charitable Giving

If charitable giving is an important part of your life and a legacy you would like carried on by your family, set up your own donor advised fund (details on this can be found on pages 105 - 110). Put your children and grandchildren on the grant committee. Every year you can have a family meeting to discuss what causes the family wants to help. I can't think of a better "inheritance" for you to leave your family.

Note: To get more information on this and other financial topics, sign up for our monthly newsletter at www.brianfricke.com. Free to readers of this book!

IF I RAN THE COUNTRY FOR A DAY...

Admit it, you've probably thought about what you would do if you were running the country, even for a day. Here's what I would do along with explanations of why I would only need one day.

RULE NO. 1

You can't change any of the other rules I put into place – ever! Don't forget this rule! In no particular order, here are the other changes I would make:

Ban Attorneys from Holding Office

If you hold any type of public office, from city commissioner up to President of the United States or you want to run for public office, you can't be an attorney, studying to be an attorney, or be a retired attorney.

Since most of our public officials are attorneys—and they've made a mess of things—I figure this group should no longer be allowed to make any more messes. We may lose a few talented leaders, but that's a risk I'm willing to take.

Fix the Tax Law

Anyone holding Public Office MUST file his or her own personal and/or business tax returns *by hand* using only the IRS provided instruction booklets. No computers, software or accountants can be used. I would hope that this would quickly lead to reform of the awful tax code. I would suggest a national sales tax. For more information go to www.fairtax.org.

Ban Special Interest Groups

If you're going to campaign for a public office, you will receive a fixed amount of money to finance your election or re-election campaign from the government. The funds will be allotted, according to the office you're seeking. Using your own money or contributions from anyone would be a felony. This policy would elminate special interest and lobbying groups.

If you're able to run a sound campaign, then the odds of being elected are tilted in your favor. If you make smart decisions when you're campaigning, presumably you'd make smart decisions when you're in public office.

Require Public Service

Anyone whose annual pay, including salary, bonuses, stock options, etc., exceeds $5 million MUST serve in a public office for a minimum of four years and no more than eight years in order to cash in on any pay in excess of $5 million. During the period of public service, the person would receive no salary.

This country needs more smart people making business-like decisions in the government. If you're sharp enough to be paid an outrageous salary, then you should be able to make capabable decisions for the good of the entire nation. Since special interest groups would no longer exist, there would be no advantage to you to push policies that would line your own pockets.

You Can't Cash Your Paycheck Until You Are Financially Literate

Basic financial education would be a requirement in every public and private school. In fact, you would not be allowed to cash your first paycheck until you complete the required course. This rule applies to high school students working part-time.

If you have to take a written test and demonstrate your skills in order to get a driver's license, there should be a similar requirement that you have certain money management skills when you start earning money. We all know a car can be a dangerous weapon in the hands of the wrong person, especially someone with no training. I believe money—especially credit cards—in the hands of someone with no basic financial training can be much more damaging than most minor automobile accidents.

Eliminate Hidden Fees

All investment companies (brokerage firms, mutual funds, banks, insurance companies, 401k plans, etc.) would be required to tell you in plain English how much money was deducted from your account to pay for fees at least once a year.

Anyone giving you advice including financial advisors, insurance agents and stockbrokers, in addition to CPA's and attorneys, must fully disclose all income and commissions on the products they sell you. This is actually very simple but no one wants to do this. Why? If you knew the real dollar amounts you're paying for services, you would be horrified! If you're one of the people who believe you're not paying for investment advice, wake up! And shame on those companies for hiding the truth.

Wipe Out More Frivolous Lawsuits

If you (or your 1-800-sue-the-world attorney) sue someone, you're going to have to have some "skin in the game." This means that you or your attorney must put up 10% of the amount you are suing for in cold hard cash.

If you and your attorney are certain that you have a solid case, this shouldn't pose any problem. If you win, your "deposit" is returned to you. If you lose, your deposit is forfeited and it will go to the person whom you sued to help reduce the costs of his or her suit. In addition, you'll be responsible for paying all court costs as well!

These requirements should dramatically reduce the number of frivolous lawsuits clogging up our court system while still providing "relief" to anyone who has been truly harmed. Perhaps, more people would try to work out disputes amongst themselves before rushing to file a lawsuit.

These changes would probably put many attorneys out of work. But, I'm not worried about that possibility. In fact, I would sleep better because the unemployed attorneys would not be able to look for employment in public office. (See above rules.)

Stop Government Pension Plans

If you're an elected official, you are not eligible for a government pension. You can receive Social Security, like the rest of us. If this is distressing, then you should look at reforming Social Security.

Overhaul the Healthcare System

If you're an elected official, you and your family must receive your healthcare from an HMO. You must also file all your own insurance claim forms yourself, by hand, in ink! If you are dissatisfied with the level of care you receive or are frustrated with all the paperwork, I'm sure you'll figure out a way to fix it.

With the diminishing number of lawsuits, the cost of premiums should go down. (See Wipe Out Frivolous Lawsuits above.)

Dramatically Reduce the Cost of Nursing Homes

If you've been responsible with your financial affairs and purchased long-term care insurance, if your expenses ever exceed the coverage/policy limits (a minimum amount of coverage would be required) neither you nor your family would be required to spend any of your hard earned savings/assets for continued care. After all of your long-term care insurance policy benefits have been exhausted, the government will step in and make payments. (Some states are experimenting with this concept now.)

Fix Social Security

Not everyone is going to get Social Security benefits *forever*. Instead, once you've gotten what you've paid into the system, there will be a means test in place in order for you to continue receiving benefits.

It's not the government's job to take care of you. The government should lend a helping hand to those truly in need. I'm guessing Bill Gates (when he's old enough) and Warren Buffett, to name a few, aren't even going to notice their Social Security check. Folks like Gates, Buffett and other very successful millionaires should receive what they've paid to the government and that's it!

Last time I checked, the odds of me getting to run the country for the day aren't looking too good. But I'm always available should the opportunity arise!

P.S. Let me know what you think about my list. Did I leave anything out? Send your thoughts and comments to <u>info@fmcretire.com</u>.

RESOURCES

- *The Ultimate Gift by Jim Stovall*

  If you only read one book from this list this is the book to read! You won't be disappointed … I guarantee it! After you've read the book, if you don't feel that it is one of the best books that you've ever read, contact me and I'll buy it from you for twice the price you paid.

LIVING A BETTER LIFE

- *The Richest Man in Babylon by George S. Clason*

  This is the book that Annette and I read before we married. It helped us set financial rules to live by and we've never had an argument about money! There should be a law requiring everyone to read this book before they cash their first paycheck.

- *The On-Purpose Person Making: Your Life Make Sense: A Modern Parable by Kevin W. McCarthy*

  Quick read – Great exercises to help you focus in on what's really important in to you.

- *See You at the Top by Zig Ziglar*

  A classic – A must read. The book is known for the line, "If you help enough people get what they want, you'll automatically get what you want!"

- *Halftime by Bob Buford*

  If you're in a period of transition in your life or trying to figure out what to do with the rest of your life, then this book is for you.

- *The New Retirementality by Mitch Anthony*

  Read this if you prefer using money as a tool to make a life instead of dedicating your life to making money!

- *Body for Life: 12 Weeks to Mental and Physical Strength by Bill Phillips*

  This is the system I used to lose 25 lbs…and I've kept the weight off.

- *How to be Like Rich DeVos: Succeeding with Integrity in Business and Life by Pat Williams and Jim Denney*

  This billionaire didn't let wealth corrupt his life and he used his success to improve the lives of others. Reading this completely changed my view of the man.

- *The Fred Factor: How Passion in your work and life can turn the ordinary into the extraordinary by Mark Sanborn*

  This book offers four principles to help bring fresh energy and creativity to your life and work.

- *The Millionaire Next Door: The Surprising Secrets of America's Wealthy by Thomas J. Stanley and William D. Danko*

  This book offers a detailed look at the habits of self-made millionaires.

- *Life 2.0: How People Across America Are Transforming Their Lives by Finding the Where of Their Happiness by Rich Karlgaard*

  Tired of your job? Been downsized or laid off? Real life examples of options you don't even realize are open to you will make you stretch your mind and broaden the horizons of your life.

- *Today God Is First, by O.S. Hillman*

  This book is my favorite daily devotional. Give it a try. I think you'll like it.

MONEY AND INVESTING

- *Values-Based Financial Planning: The Art of Creating an Inspiring Financial Strategy by Bill Bachrach*

  This book comes very close to matching our firm's approach to financial planning. The author is a friend and advisor/consultant to our firm. Read pages 79 – 86.

- *Point & Figure Charting: The Essential Application for Forecasting and Tracking Market Prices by Thomas J. Dorsey*

  This volume provides a detailed explanation of our supply and demand investment system.

- *The New Era of Wealth: How Investors Can Profit from the Five Economic Trends Shaping the Future by Brian S. Wesbury*

  This author is our favorite economist who has been named as one of the country's top ten economists by *USA Today* and *The Wall Street Journal.* We've been fortunate to have him speak to our clients on numerous occasions.

- *Everything You Know about Investing Is Wrong by John K. Sosnowy with Kori S. Voorhees*

  The book explains why dollar cost averaging doesn't work with large accounts and why traditional asset allocation doesn't work.

BUSINESS

- *Raving Fans: A Revolutionary Approach to Customer Service by Ken Blanchard and Sheldon Bowles*

  This is a must read for every business owner. It explains how to turn satisfied customers/clients into "raving fans."

- *The E Myth Revisited: Why Most Small Businesses Don't Work and What to Do About It by Michael E. Gerber*

  A business owner's must read! The book shows how to make sure your business supports the way of life you desire and not take over your life.

- *Million Dollar Consulting: The Professional Guide to Growing a Practice by Alan Weiss*

  This author provides valuable information for everyone who is or is thinking about becoming a consultant.

MORE WORRY FREE RETIREMENT!

Would you like to stay current on changes
that will affect your retirement?

FREE Resources:
Go to www.BrianFricke.com to claim your copy
of *9 Ways Retiree's Screw Up Their Finances
and How To Avoid Them* – a $47 value and
my Monthly newsletter – a $24.95 value.

You can reach me at:

**Brian Fricke, CFP
bfricke@fmcretire.com
1-800-393-1017**

To your continued success towards your
own Worry Free Retirement.